The Wadsworth Casebook Series
for Reading, Research, and Writing

A Collection of Poems

Robert Frost

THE WADSWORTH CASEBOOK SERIES
FOR READING, RESEARCH, AND WRITING

Series Editors: Laurie G. Kirszner & Stephen R. Mandell

FICTION

Edgar Allan Poe
The Cask of Amontillado

Raymond Carver
Cathedral

William Faulkner
A Rose for Emily

John Updike
A & P

Flannery O'Connor
A Good Man Is Hard to Find

Eudora Welty
A Worn Path

Charlotte Perkins Gilman
The Yellow Wallpaper

DRAMA

Susan Glaspell
Trifles

William Shakespeare
Hamlet

Athol Fugard
"Master Harold" . . . and the boys

POETRY

Robert Frost
A Collection of Poems

Emily Dickinson
A Collection of Poems

Langston Hughes
A Collection of Poems

Walt Whitman
A Collection of Poems

The Wadsworth Casebook Series
for Reading, Research, and Writing

A Collection of Poems
Robert Frost

Contributing Editor

Robert C. Peterson
Middle Tennessee State University

Series Editors

Laurie G. Kirszner
University of the Sciences in Philadelphia

Stephen R. Mandell
Drexel University

THOMSON

WADSWORTH

Australia Canada Mexico Singapore Spain United Kingdom United States

THOMSON

WADSWORTH

The Wadsworth Casebook Series for Reading, Research, and Writing
Robert Frost, *A Collection of Poems*

Publisher: *Michael Rosenberg*
Senior Editor: *Aron Keesbury*
Developmental Editor: *Marita Sermolins*
Production Editor: *Samantha Ross*
Marketing Manager: *Carrie Brandon*
Senior Print Buyer: *Mary Beth Hennebury*
Compositor: *Publishers' Design and Production Services*
Photography Manager: *Sheri Blaney*
Cover/Text Designer: *Linda Beaupré*
Printer: *West Group*

Cover Image: © *Art Explosion*

Printed in the United States of America.
1 2 3 4 5 6 7 8 9 10   07 06 05 04 03

For more information contact Wadsworth, 25 Thomson Place, Boston, MA 02210 USA, or you can visit our Internet site at http://www.wadsworth.com

ISBN: 1-4130-0044-4

Library of Congress Control Number: 2003111564

About the Series

The Wadsworth Casebook Series for Reading, Research, and Writing has its origins in our anthology *Literature: Reading, Reacting, Writing* (Fifth Edition, 2004), which in turn arose out of our many years of teaching college writing and literature courses. The primary purpose of each Casebook in the series is to offer students a convenient, self-contained reference tool that they can use to gain insight into a work (or works) of literature and to complete a research project for an introductory literature course.

In choosing subjects for the Casebooks, we drew on our own experience in the classroom, selecting works of poetry, fiction, and drama that students like to read, discuss, and write about and that teachers like to teach. Unlike other collections of literary criticism aimed at students, the Wadsworth Casebook Series for Reading, Research, and Writing features short stories, groups of poems, or plays (rather than longer works, such as novels) because these are the genres most often taught in college-level Introduction to Literature courses. In selecting particular authors and titles, we focus on those most frequently assigned and those most accessible to students.

To facilitate student research—and to facilitate instructor supervision of that research—each Casebook contains all the resources students need to produce a documented research paper on a particular work of literature. Every Casebook in the series includes the following elements:

- A comprehensive **introduction** to the work, providing a social, historical, and political background. This introduction helps students to understand the work and the author in the context of a particular time and place. In particular, the introduction enables students to appreciate customs, events, and ideas that may have contributed to the author's choice of subject matter, emphasis, or style.
- **About the Author,** a biographical discussion that includes information such as the author's birth and death dates; details of the work's first publication and its subsequent publication history, if

relevant; details about the author's life; a summary of the author's career; and a discussion of key published works.

- The most widely accepted version of the **literary work,** along with the explanatory footnotes students will need to understand unfamiliar terms and concepts or references to people, places, or events.

- **Discussion questions** focusing on themes developed in the work. These questions, designed to stimulate critical thinking and discussion, can also serve as springboards for research projects.

- A list of topics for extended **research assignments** related to the literary work. Students may use these assignments exactly as they appear in the Casebook, or students or instructors may modify the assignments to suit their own needs or research interests.

- A diverse collection of traditional and nontraditional **secondary sources,** which may include scholarly articles, reviews, interviews, memoirs, newspaper articles, historical documents, and so on, as well as photographs and other visuals. This resource offers students access to sources they might not turn to on their own—for example, a popular song that inspired a short story, a story that was the original version of a play, a legal document that sheds light on a work's theme, or two different biographies of an author—thus encouraging students to look beyond the obvious or the familiar as they search for ideas. Students may use only these sources, or they may supplement them with sources listed in the Casebook's bibliography (see below).

- An annotated model **student research paper** drawing on several of the Casebook's secondary sources. This paper uses MLA parenthetical documentation and includes a Works Cited list conforming to MLA style.

- A comprehensive **bibliography** of print and electronic sources related to the work. This bibliography offers students an opportunity to move beyond the sources in the Casebook to other sources related to a particular research topic.

- A concise, up-to-date **guide to MLA documentation,** including information on what kinds of information require documentation (and what kinds do not); a full explanation of how to construct parenthetical references and how to place them in a paper; sample parenthetical reference formats for various kinds of sources used in papers about literature; a complete explanation of how to assemble a works-cited list accompanied by sample works-cited entries (including formats for documenting electronic sources); and guidelines for using explanatory notes (with examples).

By collecting all this essential information in one convenient place, each volume in the Wadsworth Casebook Series for Reading, Research, and Writing responds to the needs of both students and teachers. For students, the Casebooks offer convenience, referentiality, and portability, making the process of doing research easier. For instructors, the Casebooks offer the flexibility and control necessary to teach students how to use sources when writing about literature. For example, teachers may choose to assign one Casebook or more than one; thus, they have the option of having all students in a class write about the same work or having different groups of students, or individual students, write about different works. In addition, instructors may ask students to use only the secondary sources collected in the Casebook, thereby controlling students' use of (and acknowledgment of) sources more closely, or they may encourage students to seek sources (both print and electronic) beyond those included in the Casebook. By building convenience, structure, and flexibility into each volume, we have designed the Wadsworth Casebook Series for Reading, Research, and Writing to suit a wide variety of teaching styles and research interests. The Casebooks have made the research paper an easier project for us and a less stressful one for our students; we hope they will do the same for you.

Laurie G. Kirszner
Stephen R. Mandell
Series Editors

Preface

Robert Frost: A Collection of Poems offers a sampling of the poetry that Frost wrote throughout a career that lasted over half a century. Some of the poems here are familiar, and others are less familiar. This selection introduces readers to crucial elements in Frost's work: his interest in New England, in nature and the relationship of human beings to it, and in poetry as a way of knowing about the world and oneself. Frost is an iconic figure in American literature, chiefly because of his own efforts to project himself onto the times in which he lived and wrote. Seeing beyond the public man can help readers understand his achievement as a poet.

Assessing Frost's contribution to American literature has preoccupied readers and critics for several generations, and although the general consensus is that he is a major poet, it is not clear just why that is the case. Frost the public man, the one who taught at the Bread Loaf Writers' Conference and various universities for years, often gets in the way of his own work. He wrote provocative essays, gave interviews in which he made controversial statements, and enjoyed stirring up other people's settled convictions. The effect of all this was positive in many cases, but for some readers, the public Frost inhabits the poems. His work's very familiarity also makes it hard for readers to see it clearly. The frequently anthologized and quoted poems overshadow the fuller range of Frost's work, and while a popular poem like "Birches" does have a kind of thematic and technical perfection, that very fact misrepresents Frost's more typical achievement. As a whole, his poetry stands in opposition to the technical experimentation of literary modernism. Thus it shows how much Frost wanted to confront prevailing literary dogma and reveals how conservative his values were.

This Casebook assumes you will come to grips with Frost's poetry for yourself, as you also become aware of the variety of critical responses to his work. The secondary sources here are intended to help you do just that. Some of them will help you understand Frost's own thinking about poetry, and others will offer readings of individual poems or groups of poems from slightly different critical perspectives. These materials are not here to do your thinking for you, and you are not expected to agree with everything said in them. Read the poems reproduced here, read other poems by Frost if you like, and reach your own conclusions about what he has to say and how he goes about saying it. Brief descriptions of these secondary materials follow:

- Frost, Robert. "The Figure a Poem Makes" and "Poetry and School." These essays reflect Frost's thinking about poetry in general and about his own work in particular. The first, written as the preface for the 1939 edition of his *Collected Poems*, was one of Frost's favorites.

- Bracker, Milton. "He Himself is Perhaps the Biggest Metaphor of All." Originally published in the *New York Times Magazine* in 1958, this interview catches Frost in a particularly reflective mood. Bracker's profile describes the poet's appearance and manner accurately, and Frost answers questions about his work and that of other writers with characteristic frankness.

- Conder, John J. " 'After Apple-Picking': Frost's Troubled Sleep." In this essay, Conder offers a thorough reading of a single well-known poem. He suggests that this poem is central to an understanding of Frost's work, and he tackles the problem of reading beyond the literal narrative.

- Bidney, Martin. "The Secretive-Playful Epiphanies of Robert Frost: Solitude, Companionship, and the Ambivalent Imagination." In this excerpt Bidney proposes a hypothesis about certain of Frost's poems about nature. The thematic focus of this selection may help a reader connect one poem with others.

- Greiner, Donald J. " 'That Plain-Speaking Guy': A Conversation with James Dickey on Robert Frost." Dickey and Greiner, talking during the centennial celebration of Frost's birth, attempt to separate the man from his work and to assess his achievement. Since Dickey himself is a poet, his reactions to Frost are particularly interesting.

- Meredith, William. "In Memory of Robert Frost." A friend and fellow poet, Meredith offers insight into his relationship with Frost and writes about important features of the poet's personality.

Following these materials is a sample student research paper using MLA documentation style. In this paper, Pablo Tanguay offers a reading of two of the poems reprinted in the Casebook. He uses some of the secondary sources provided here as well as another source. Note that throughout his essay, the student writer is careful to subordinate the researched materials to his own thesis and to keep the focus on the poems themselves and his own response to them.

Acknowledgments

A number of remarkable people have contributed to this Casebook project, and without their help, there would be no *Robert Frost: A Collection of Poems*. I would like to thank the Series Editors Laurie Kirszner and Stephen Mandell. Being associated with their anthology *Literature: Reading, Reacting, Writing* is a real pleasure. I would also like to thank all those at Wadsworth who worked with me on the Casebook. It was Aron Keesbury, the Senior Development Editor, who broached the project to me, but Marita Sermolins, English Editorial Assistant, has given me guidance and help all the way, and I appreciate her work. It has made this so much more fun to do. I would also like to thank my friend and student Pablo Tanguay, who took on the assignment of drafting a student essay for the project and did it skillfully and well. Finally, let me salute the memory of the late Robert Liddell Lowe, Professor of English at Purdue University. Many, many years ago, Professor Lowe took me through graduate courses in Romantic, Victorian, and Modern poetry that kindled my enthusiasm for the genre.

Robert C. Peterson
Contributing Editor

Contents

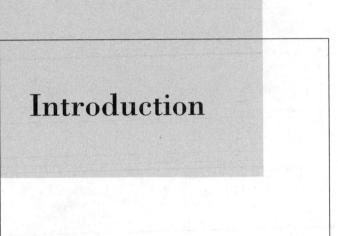

Introduction

Robert Frost and Modern Poetry

When Robert Frost wrote in an essay entitled "Poetry and School," originally published in the *Atlantic Monthly* in 1951, "For my pleasure I had as soon write free verse as play tennis with the net down" (38), he was doing more than indulging his taste for saying slightly controversial things. By this stage in his life, Frost was a public figure, somebody known beyond the relatively enclosed world of those reading and writing poetry. In 1954, he made a US-government sponsored trip to Brazil; he made a similar trip to England in 1957, where he received honorary degrees from Oxford and Cambridge Universities and from the National University of Ireland. After reading his poem "The Gift Outright" at the inauguration of President John F. Kennedy in 1961, he made a trip sponsored by the State Department to Russia in 1962 (Potter xvi).

Robert Frost reading "The Gift Outright," 1961.

When he returned to the United States in September, Frost told reporters that Premier Nikita " 'Kruschev said we were too liberal to fight' " (qtd. in Parini 434). He thereby stuck his oar into the delicate relationship between the Soviet Union and the United States that climaxed six weeks later with the Cuban Missile Crisis. The incident reveals a great deal about the man. Robert Frost had opinions, chiefly conservative ones where politics and literature were concerned, and he did not hesitate to voice them. In this, he was characteristically American.

Frost was probably telling the truth when he said he would just as soon play tennis without a net as write free verse. The statement suggests something about his relationship with his modernist contemporaries T. S. Eliot and Ezra Pound, men to whom he owed thanks for help in launching his career as a published poet. It also suggests something about Frost's own ideas about poetry. He writes in that *Atlantic Monthly* essay, "Poetry plays the rhythms of dramatic speech on the grid of meter. A good map carries its own scale of miles" ("Poetry and School" 38). Clearly, Frost saw a fruitful tension between the rhythm of conversational speech and that of strict meter, and this understanding prevented him from abandoning traditional metrical features for what seemed to him the formlessness of free verse. Richard Poirier notes that Frost "consciously excluded himself" (39) from the sort of modernism typified by James Joyce and T. S. Eliot and suggests that there were a number of reasons for this: psychological, historical, and literary. "It was not that Joyce and Eliot," Poirier observes, "were mythologizing the century and that Frost was not; it is rather that they exhibit different mythologies about the possibilities and functions of literature *in* the century." He continues, "Curiously enough, Frost's belief in the personal salvation made possible by the assertion of form was a function of his *dis*belief in the capacity of form to do much more than that" (44). Where Frost was clearly of his time and responsive to the social and literary conditions in which he lived, he was not in the mainstream of literary modernism.

FROST AND THE DEVELOPMENT
OF MODERN POETRY

There are ways in which Frost's work differs from that of his fellow American poets Ezra Pound and T. S. Eliot, and these differences reflect the relationship of each poet's work to the development of modern poetry in English. Defining modernism is not an easy task; books have been written on the subject. Nevertheless, one basic characteristic of modernism is replacing mimetic realism by a concept of representation that implied that "instead of copying the external world [,] the work could render it in an image insisting on its own distinctive form of reality" (*The New Princeton Encyclopedia* 793). Where T. S. Eliot's poem "The Love Song of J. Alfred Prufrock" (1915) describes the interior landscape of its persona's mind more than it does the cityscape of contemporary London, Frost's poems in *A Boy's Will* (1913) and *North of Boston* (1914), while very much concerned with emotional and even spiritual consciousness, seem much more firmly rooted in a real place and time. Eliot and Pound, the latter in a poem such as "Hugh Selwyn Mauberley" (1920), "develop collage techniques" for intensifying the "formal patternings" of images in their texts, thereby creating poems in which "the spaces between the images . . . offer the audience its access to the mode of spirit defined by the work" (*The New Princeton Encyclopedia* 793). Frost also uses images in his work, but unlike those found in Eliot's "The Waste Land" (1922), his images are subordinated to the narratives that organize poems such as "Birches" and "After Apple-Picking." Because his images—note the "long two-pointed" ladder "sticking through a tree / Toward heaven still" (1–2) in the latter poem—so often begin in a specific time and place, and as a result are literal and realistic in at least their original form, Frost positions himself in opposition to the stylistic characteristics of much of modernism. Rather than resembling the work of Pound and Eliot, Frost's work has much more in common with the poetry of Thomas Hardy, Edgar Lee Masters, and Edwin Arlington Robinson. Each poet was writing during the years when modernist aesthetics were being formulated, but they were not affected much by that style of writing.

FROST AND THE SEARCH FOR MEANING IN NATURE

Where Frost's work shows common ground with that of his peers, it occurs in the treatment of shared subject matter and themes. This may not be apparent on the surface of his poetry, for as David Perkins notes, Frost "begins with a radical self-restriction" to New England and its lifestyle. "His idiom," Perkins adds, "is educated but talked American, with a slight wash of country vocabulary and often a Yankee intonation" (227). Harold H. Watts says that most of Frost's poetry "is a dialogue in which the two speakers are Robert Frost himself and the entity which we call nature or process." Typically, Watts claims, Frost uses his poems to pose questions to that natural world and to contemplate the answers given back. "They are answers that an ethically curious person like Frost can profit by," Watts observes. "Whether he—and we—are meant to profit by them . . . is not always very important to Frost" (Watts 105).

This act of posing questions to the universe connects Frost's work to that of Thomas Hardy. "The Darkling Thrush," for example, or "The Convergence of the Twain" shows Hardy's preoccupation with the relationship of human beings and with that power that governs the natural world. The questions Hardy asks and the answers he receives may not be precisely those found in his work, but Frost's "Design" probes material that Hardy might have used. The convergence of white moth, white flower, and white spider, as phenomena that are natural but not ordinary or typical, leads Frost to end by asking if the cause of their conjunction is not "What but design of darkness to appall?— / If design govern in a thing so small" (13–14). This concern with causation, design, and the ethical qualities of nature itself links to "The Darkling Thrush," where Hardy describes a winter scene in which "An aged thrush" (21) produces a song described as "ecstatic sound" (26). The speaker says that despite evidence of it in the actual natural scene, he "could think there trembled through / His happy good-night air / Some blessed Hope, whereof he knew / And I was unaware" (29–32). Hardy's and Frost's concerns here are not unique. The work of Gerard Manley Hopkins, which appeared in a posthumous volume in 1918, also deals with perception of the universe's order through a focus on the natural world.

Both William Dean Howells and Amy Lowell linked Frost's work with that of Edgar Lee Masters (Parini 172, 188), as other contemporaries did, and some commentators saw similarities between the poetry of Frost and of Edwin Arlington Robinson (Poirier 229–32). Frost himself resisted these comparisons, for while both Masters and Robinson were realists, poets focused on a region of America, and traditionalists in style and technique, their work does not resonate the way Frost's does. Nevertheless, there are things linking their work to his. For example, Masters, Robinson, and Frost all celebrate American identity. Pieces from *Spoon River Anthology* (1915) like Masters' "Lucinda Matlock" and "Ann Rutledge" reveal a tenacity and love for life not unlike that to be found in Frost's "Wild Grapes" and "Two Look at Two." Robinson's "Eros Turannos" shares with Frost's "The Hill Wife" an awareness of the pain associated with human love and its potential sadness. There is darkness in the work of all three poets that, on the surface, makes them seem similar.

This dark quality in Frost's work did not receive much attention until the Columbia University celebration of the poet's seventy-fifth birthday in 1959, when Lionel Trilling described Frost as a "'terrifying poet.'" (qtd. in Poirier 3). Richard Poirier says, "Trilling was proposing that Frost was radical in a classic American tradition." He explains that Trilling pointed out that "Frost was trying to slough off an old inherited European consciousness in order that a new consciousness could come to life from underneath" (5).

This impulse in Frost links him squarely with an element of nineteenth-century American literature usually described as Transcendentalism. Eric Link notes that critics see a connection between Frost's work and that of Ralph Waldo Emerson and Henry David Thoreau (182), a connection that a number of Frost's own statements seem to demonstrate. Link connects specific passages in Thoreau's *The Maine Woods* (1864) to certain texts by Frost in which he "uses, manipulates, and reconfigures similar themes" (185). Where Frost's use of nature as a subject is concerned, it may be necessary to be remember something John J. Conder says in his discussion of "After Apple-Picking": "Both Frost's habit of speaking contraries and his point of view toward nature militate against a simplistic view of sleep" (49). There is nothing simplistic about Frost's poems at all.

FROST AND AMERICAN LITERATURE
AT MID-CENTURY

By the late 1930s, Frost had emerged as a major figure in American poetry. He had been a faculty member at various universities and had toured regularly, reading his own poetry to large audiences. At the same time, his production slowed; there were longer gaps between published books. John Ogilvie argues that Frost's "'very manner of voice changes. Metaphorical indirection gives way to explicit generalization'" (qtd. in Bidney 270). The popular response to Frost increased from this point in his career. There may have been a degree of sentimentality in this reaction: with the start of World War II, and later during the Cold War, readers turned to subjects that recalled simpler and happier times. James Guimond, on a Web site maintained at Georgetown University, notes that students sometimes have problems understanding the values in Frost's poems. They reflect a society "that was rural, fearful of change, distrustful of technology, proud of craftsmanship, and deeply committed to privacy and self-reliance" (Guimond par. 1). It might, as a result, be easy to misunderstand what Frost says in his work because of the difference between his world and ours.

It might be equally easy to misunderstand his poems because they are so compelling on a literal level. Frost himself does not sentimentalize the rural, agricultural life he writes about. He knows that for all the pleasure to be derived from a close relationship with nature, there are costs in human feeling. Parini notes the Emersonian overtones of Frost's interest in "the relation of inner and outer worlds" in the poem "Tree at My Window" (237). "Two Look at Two" also develops complex ideas about human consciousness. The encounter between a human couple and a buck and doe, separated by a wall that constitutes a barrier between the couple and the rest of nature, clearly illustrates Frost's acknowledgement of the difficulty human beings have in understanding the world in which they exist. The man and woman, walking up a mountain near the end of daylight, reach that barrier and cast "one last look the way they must not go" (10). Beyond the wall is a "failing path, where, if a stone / Or earthslide moved at night, it moved itself" (11–12). They have reached the point at which the natural world separates itself from the human. While they project their consciousness across that wall, personifying the deer and giving them speech and human feelings, that is only what it is—a projection, something of the Emersonian sort perhaps, for doesn't he argue in "Nature" that idea is the ultimate reality? The buck "jerks" his head, "[a]s if to ask" (31, 32) why the humans do not move. " 'I doubt if you're as living as you look' " (34), the couple hear him saying. These words, of course, are not the buck's; they are words put in his mouth by the couple looking at him; more precisely, they are the words of the poem's speaker, who enters into the consciousness of each of the participants.

Something like what Martin Bidney calls a "a playful epiphany" takes place in this poem. He defines the phrase as "conceptual tension, an emotional ambivalence" in which the question to be answered is whether the situation being examined is "a revelation or a mere frivolity" (54). Frost ends the poem in a way that seems to affirm the genuineness of the moment. The couple stand there after the deer have passed, "A great wave from it going over them, / As if the earth in one unlooked-for favor / Had made them certain earth returned their love" (40–42). But that "as if" signals clearly that the statement reveals only the subjective consciousness of the human pair. What they feel may be true, of course. There may be no way to tell, but Frost seems to say that where the natural world is patterned and orderly, human thought processes have trouble understanding and explaining it.

FROST'S ACHIEVEMENT AS A WRITER

It is in terms of ideas like this that Frost's poetry embodies American poetry at the middle of the twentieth century. The poet James Dickey says, "The Frost I like is the plain-speaking guy who can in the most conversational possible way say things that you wouldn't have thought of in a million years" (qtd. in Greiner 67). In a conversation with Donald J. Greiner, Dickey identifies the qualities he likes best in Frost's poetry and lists the poems he thinks are Frost's best. Both men think that the public image of Frost, the persona he created as teacher and lecturer, prevents people from seeing Frost's achievement as a writer (63). Dickey says that "the thing about Frost that makes him so good is that he's able to say the most amazing things without seeming to raise his voice" (qtd. in Greiner 65). Others may have different explanations for Frost's staying power, but there is no question that he has survived his generation and that people continue to read his poems and to take them seriously.

One cannot look at American poetry in the first half of the twentieth century without coming to terms with the work of Robert Frost. "The poetry itself," Parini concludes, "is marked by an unbelievable, even visionary, clarity" (441). It also evokes the reality of a particular place (Parini 447), of a real part of the United States made metaphoric by his treatment. Poirier says that Frost is "of vital interest and consequence because his ultimate subject is the interpretive process itself" (xi). His poems both are about knowing and are themselves a way of understanding what it is to be human. "They cannot scare me with their empty spaces / Between stars," the speaker in "Desert Places" asserts, when he has the capacity "To scare myself with my own desert spaces" (13–14, 16). Tempting as it might be to look at this poem, and others by Frost, as reflections of his own psychological situation, to do so might diminish its power. What Frost is talking about is a human feeling we can all share, and this feeling of universality happens for at least two reasons. The first is that his poems are metaphors. That is, they are about literal experiences that Frost handles in such a way that their meaning becomes figurative. The second is that his poems are crafted meticulously. They have to be read aloud, for their meaning comes from this. It is necessary to hear the voice of the persona in each Frost poem; a reader must hear and feel the rhythms of the lines, inhabit the world each poem evokes, and experience the moment that each poem captures. When Frost gets these things right, his poems resonate in the mind.

WORKS CITED

Bidney, Martin. "The Secretive-Playful Epiphanies of Robert Frost: Solitude, Companionship, and the Ambivalent Imagination." The Wadsworth Casebook for Reading, Research, and Writing: Robert Frost: A Collection of Poems. Ed. Robert C. Petersen. Boston: Wadsworth, 2004. 54–62.

Conder, John J. "'After Apple-Picking': Frost's Troubled Sleep." The Wadsworth Casebook for Reading, Research, and Writing: Robert Frost: A Collection of Poems. Ed. Robert C. Petersen. Boston: Wadsworth, 2004. 44–53.

Frost, Robert. "After Apple-Picking." The Wadsworth Casebook for Reading, Research, and Writing: Robert Frost: A Collection of Poems. Ed. Robert C. Petersen. Boston: Wadsworth, 2004. 20–21.

———. "Desert Places." The Wadsworth Casebook for Reading, Research, and Writing: Robert Frost: A Collection of Poems. Ed. Robert C. Petersen. Boston: Wadsworth, 2004. 26.

———. "Design." The Wadsworth Casebook for Reading, Research, and Writing: Robert Frost: A Collection of Poems. Ed. Robert C. Petersen. Boston: Wadsworth, 2004. 26.

———. "Poetry and School." The Wadsworth Casebook for Reading, Research, and Writing: Robert Frost: A Collection of Poems. Ed. Robert C. Petersen. Boston: Wadsworth, 2004. 35–38.

———. "Two Look at Two." The Wadsworth Casebook for Reading, Research, and Writing: Robert Frost: A Collection of Poems. Ed. Robert C. Petersen. Boston: Wadsworth, 2004. 24–25.

Greiner, Donald J. "'That Plain-Speaking Guy': A Conversation with James Dickey on Robert Frost." The Wadsworth Casebook for Reading, Research, and Writing: Robert Frost: A Collection of Poems. Ed. Robert C. Petersen. Boston: Wadsworth, 2004. 62–70.

Guimond, James. Robert Frost (1874–1963). Georgetown University. 25 June 2003 <http://www.georgetown.edufaculty/bassr/heath/syllabuild/iguide/frost.html>.

Hardy, Thomas. "The Darkling Thrush." The Complete Poems of Thomas Hardy. Ed. James Gibson. New York: Macmillan, 1976. 150.

Link, Eric Carl. "Nature's Extra-Vagrants: Frost and Thoreau in the Maine Woods." Papers on Language and Literature 33.2 (1997): 182–97.

The New Princeton Encyclopedia of Poetry and Poetics. Ed. Alex Preminger and T. V. F. Brogan. Princeton, NJ: Princeton UP, 1993.

Parini, Jay. Robert Frost: A Life. New York: Holt, 1999.

Perkins, David. "Robert Frost." A History of Modern Poetry: From the 1890s to Pound, Eliot, and Yeats. Cambridge: Harvard UP, 1976. 227–51.

Poirier, Richard. Robert Frost: The Work of Knowing. New York: Oxford UP, 1977.

Potter, James L. Robert Frost Handbook. University Park: Pennsylvania State UP, 1980.

Watts, Harold H. "Robert Frost and the Interrupted Dialogue." Robert Frost: A Collection of Critical Essays. Ed. James M. Cox. Englewood Cliffs, NJ: Prentice Hall, 1962. 105–22.

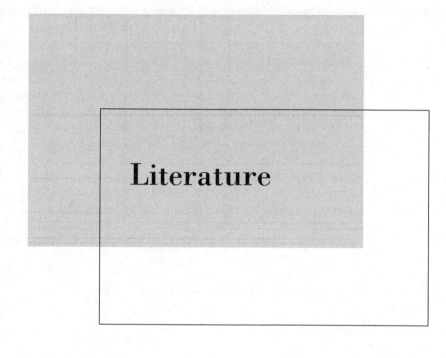

Literature

About the Author:
Robert Frost

R obert Frost (1874–1963) may be the best known American poet of the twentieth century. Born in San Francisco, where he lived until he was eleven years old, he is nevertheless associated with New England, and in particular with Vermont and New Hampshire. That association is due to Frost's work as a poet; *A Boy's Will* (1913), his first published book, takes New England's people, history, and geography as his most characteristic subject. It is also due to the public persona Frost created as teacher, public speaker, and reader of his own poetry. An actual farmer for a number of years, he made himself into a country philosopher poet, a gruff, witty spokesman for conservative social and literary positions.

Frost graduated from high school in Lawrence, Massachusetts, and attended Dartmouth College for a single semester. He then worked in a factory for a time, taught elementary school, and married high school classmate Elinor White in 1895. Two years later, he entered Harvard University; he left in 1899 and never finished an undergraduate degree. This initiated Frost's ten-year period as a farmer in Derry, New Hampshire; from time to time, he taught school, and in 1911, Frost joined the faculty of the New Hampshire State Normal School in Plymouth. Throughout this stage of his life, he wrote steadily, but other than a scattering of individual poems, he was not able to find a publisher for his work. It was after Frost decided to move his entire family to England in 1912 that his career got started, partly through the help of his fellow American poet Ezra Pound, with the British publication of *A Boy's Will* and *North of Boston* (1914). Despite his association with Pound and T. S. Eliot, another expatriate American poet, his friendship with the Irish poet William Butler Yeats, and publication in Harriet Monroe's magazine *Poetry* in Chicago, Frost was a modern writer but no modernist. His subject matter was too realistic and his technique as a poet too traditional.

The advent of World War I in Europe sent the Frost family back to the United States and eventually to a farm in Franconia, New Hampshire. The publisher Henry Holt reissued the two volumes of poems originally published in England and followed them with *Mountain Interval* (1916). Holt remained Frost's American publisher for the rest of his career. In 1917, Frost started teaching at Amherst College, the first of a series of appointments as a teacher of poetry and writer-in-residence that eventually took him to the University of Michigan, Harvard University, and Dartmouth College. He joined the faculty of the Bread Loaf School of English in Vermont in the summer of 1921 and remained associated with the school on and off for the rest of his life.

Starting in the late 1920s, Frost began to receive a steady stream of honors. His volume *New Hampshire* received a Pulitzer Prize for poetry in 1924, the first of four such awards, the others following in 1931, 1937, and 1943. He started collecting honorary doctoral degrees, eventually receiving more than twenty-five, from institutions such as Middlebury, Yale University, Oxford and Cambridge Universities, and the University of California. Frost was elected to the American Institute of Arts and Letters in 1916 and received its Gold Medal for Poetry in 1939. He was the guest of honor at the White House for a celebration of his eightieth birthday in 1954. Frost received a Gold Medal for Distinguished Service from the Poetry Society of America in 1958, and in the same year, he was appointed Consultant in Poetry (now Poet Laureate) at the Library of Congress. In 1961, he was asked to participate in the inauguration of President John F. Kennedy, reading "The Gift Outright" as part of the ceremony. In 1962, he received a Congressional Gold Medal from President Kennedy, an award recommended by President Eisenhower. The following year, he received the Bollingen Prize in Poetry.

By the time of his death, Frost had become a popular figure, known for his teaching, his public readings, and his interviews. The traditional nature of his subject matter appealed to an American public that was no longer rural and that had faced the challenges of the Great Depression, World War II, and the Cold War. Some contemporary readers had difficulty seeing beyond Frost's persona and recognizing that his work does more than reflect traditional values such as self-reliance. Lionel Trilling was not alone in seeing a darker side to Frost's poetry, but his remarks at the poet's eighty-fifth birthday celebration in New York set the agenda for discussion of Frost's work for two decades. We now look at the way in which Frost's poems depict human isolation, the limits to human understanding of nature, and

Robert Frost, 1913.

people's efforts to explain the meaning of life itself. We also look at Frost's poems as examples of traditional craftsmanship. His work reveals that he is a master of rhythm and tone, that he has the ability to create powerful dramatic situations, and that he can craft lines that stick in our memories.

Mending Wall

(1914)

Something there is that doesn't love a wall,
That sends the frozen-ground-swell under it,
And spills the upper boulders in the sun;
And makes gaps even two can pass abreast.
The work of hunters is another thing: 5
I have come after them and made repair
Where they have left not one stone on a stone,
But they would have the rabbit out of hiding,
To please the yelping dogs. The gaps I mean,
No one has seen them made or heard them made,   10
But at spring mending-time we find them there.
I let my neighbor know beyond the hill;
And on a day we meet to walk the line
And set the wall between us once again.
We keep the wall between us as we go.   15
To each the boulders that have fallen to each.
And some are loaves and some so nearly balls
We have to use a spell to make them balance:
'Stay where you are until our backs are turned!'
We wear our fingers rough with handling them.   20
Oh just another kind of outdoor game,
One on a side. It comes to little more:
There where it is we do not need the wall:
He is all pine and I am apple orchard.
My apple trees will never get across   25
And eat the cones under his pines, I tell him.
He only says, 'Good fences make good neighbors.'
Spring is the mischief in me, and I wonder
If I could put a notion in his head:
'*Why* do they make good neighbors? Isn't it   30

Where there are cows? But here there are no cows.
Before I built a wall I'd ask to know
What I was walling in or walling out,
And to whom I was like to give offense.
Something there is that doesn't love a wall,   35
That wants it down.' I could say 'Elves' to him,
But it's not elves exactly, and I'd rather
He said it for himself. I see him there
Bringing a stone grasped firmly by the top
In each hand, like an old-stone savage armed.   40
He moves in darkness as it seems to me,
Not of woods only and the shade of trees.
He will not go behind his father's saying,
And he likes having thought of it so well
He says again, 'Good fences make good neighbors.'   45

After Apple-Picking

(1914)

My long two-pointed ladder's sticking through a tree
Toward heaven still,
And there's a barrel that I didn't fill
Beside it, and there may be two or three
Apples I didn't pick upon some bough.   5
But I am done with apple-picking now.
Essence of winter sleep is on the night,
The scent of apples: I am drowsing off.
I cannot rub the strangeness from my sight
I got from looking through a pane of glass   10
I skimmed this morning from the drinking trough
And held against the world of hoary grass.
It melted, and I let it fall and break.
But I was well
Upon my way to sleep before it fell,   15
And I could tell
What form my dreaming was about to take.
Magnified apples appear and disappear,
Stem end and blossom end,

And every fleck of russet showing clear. 20
My instep arch not only keeps the ache,
It keeps the pressure of a ladder-round.
I feel the ladder sway as the boughs bend.
And I keep hearing from the cellar bin
The rumbling sound 25
Of load on load of apples coming in.
For I have had too much
Of apple-picking: I am overtired
Of the great harvest I myself desired.
There were ten thousand thousand fruit to touch, 30
Cherish in hand, lift down, and not let fall.
For all
That struck the earth,
No matter if not bruised or spiked with stubble,
Went surely to the cider-apple heap 35
As of no worth.
One can see what will trouble
This sleep of mine, whatever sleep it is.
Were he not gone,
The woodchuck could say whether it's like his 40
Long sleep, as I describe it coming on,
Or just some human sleep.

The Road Not Taken

(1915)

Two roads diverged in a yellow wood,
And sorry I could not travel both
And be one traveler, long I stood
And looked down one as far as I could
To where it bent in the undergrowth; 5

Then took the other, as just as fair,
And having perhaps the better claim,
Because it was grassy and wanted wear;
Though as for that the passing there
Had worn them really about the same, 10

And both that morning equally lay
In leaves no step had trodden black.
Oh, I kept the first for another day!
Yet knowing how way leads on to way,
I doubted if I should ever come back.   15

I shall be telling this with a sigh
Somewhere ages and ages hence:
Two roads diverged in a wood, and I—
I took the one less traveled by,
And that has made all the difference.   20

Birches

(1915)

When I see birches bend to left and right
Across the lines of straighter darker trees,
I like to think some boy's been swinging them.
But swinging doesn't bend them down to stay
As ice-storms do. Often you must have seen them   5
Loaded with ice a sunny winter morning
After the rain. They click upon themselves
As the breeze rises, and turn many-colored
As the stir cracks and crazes their enamel.
Soon the sun's warmth makes them shed crystal shells   10
Shattering and avalanching on the snow-crust—
Such heaps of broken glass to sweep away
You'd think the inner dome of heaven had fallen.
They are dragged to the withered bracken by the load,
And they seem not to break; though once they are bowed   15
So low for long, they never right themselves:
You may see their trunks arching in the woods
Years afterwards, trailing their leaves on the ground
Like girls on hands and knees that throw their hair
Before them over their heads to dry in the sun.   20
But I was going to say when Truth broke in

With all her matter-of-fact about the ice-storm
I should prefer to have some boy bend them
As he went out and in to fetch the cows—
Some boy too far from town to learn baseball,   25
Whose only play was what he found himself,
Summer or winter, and could play alone.
One by one he subdued his father's trees
By riding them down over and over again
Until he took the stiffness out of them,   30
And not one but hung limp, not one was left
For him to conquer. He learned all there was
To learn about not launching too soon
And so not carrying the tree away
Clear to the ground. He always kept his poise   35
To the top branches, climbing carefully
With the same pains you use to fill a cup
Up to the brim, and even above the brim.
Then he flung outward, feet first, with a swish,
Kicking his way down through the air to the ground.   40
So was I once myself a swinger of birches.
And so I dream of going back to be.
It's when I'm weary of considerations,
And life is too much like a pathless wood
Where your face burns and tickles with the cobwebs   45
Broken across it, and one eye is weeping
From a twig's having lashed across it open.
I'd like to get away from earth awhile
And then come back to it and begin over.
May no fate willfully misunderstand me   50
And half grant what I wish and snatch me away
Not to return. Earth's the right place for love:
I don't know where it's likely to go better.
I'd like to go by climbing a birch tree,
And climb black branches up a snow-white trunk   55
Toward Heaven, till the tree could bear no more,
But dipped its top and set me down again.
That would be good both going and coming back.
One could do worse than be a swinger of birches.

Two Look at Two

(1916)

Love and forgetting might have carried them
A little further up the mountainside
With night so near, but not much further up.
They must have halted soon in any case
With thoughts of the path back, how rough it was   5
With rock and washout, and unsafe in darkness;
When they were halted by a tumbled wall
With barbed-wired binding. They stood facing this,
Spending what onward impulse they still had
In last look the way they must not go,   10
On up the failing path, where, if a stone
Or earthslide moved at night, it moved itself;
No footstep moved it. 'This is all,' they sighed,
'Good-night to woods.' But not so; there was more.
A doe from round a spruce stood looking at them   15
Across the wall, as near the wall as they.
She saw them in their field, they her in hers.
The difficulty of seeing what stood still,
Like some up-ended boulder split in two,
Was in her clouded eyes: they saw no fear there.   20
She seemed to think that two thus they were safe.
Then, as if they were something that, though strange,
She could not trouble her mind with too long,
She sighed and passed unscared along the wall.
'*This*, then, is all. What more is there to ask?'   25
But no, not yet. A snort to bid them wait.
A buck from round the spruce stood looking at them
Across the wall as near the wall as they.
This was an antlered buck of lusty nostril,
Not the same doe come back to her place.   30
He viewed them quizzically with jerks of head,
As if to ask, 'Why don't you make some motion?
Or give some sign of life? Because you can't.
I doubt if you're as living as you look.'
Thus till he had them almost feeling dared   35
To stretch a proffering hand—and a spell-breaking.

Then he too passed unscared along the wall.
Two had seen two, whichever side you spoke from.
'This *must* be all.' It was all. Still they stood,
A great wave from it going over them,   40
As if the earth in one unlooked-for favor
Had made them certain earth returned their love.

The Need of Being Versed in
Country Things

(1920)

The house had gone to bring again
To the midnight sky a sunset glow.
Now the chimney was all of the house that stood,
Like a pistil after the petals go.

The barn opposed across the way,   5
That would have joined the house in flame
Had it been the will of the wind, was left
To bear forsaken the place's name.

No more it opened with all one end
For teams that came by the stony road   10
To drum on the floor with scurrying hoofs
And brush the mow with the summer load.

The birds that came to it through the air
At broken windows flew out and in,
Their murmur more like the sigh we sigh   15
From too much dwelling on what has been.

Yet for them the lilac renewed its leaf,
And the aged elm, though touched with fire;
And the dry pump flung up an awkward arm;
And the fence post carried a strand of wire.   20

For them there was really nothing sad.
But though they rejoiced in the next they kept,
One had to be versed in country things
Not to believe the phoebes wept.

Desert Places

(1936)

Snow falling and night falling fast, oh, fast
In a field I looked into going past,
And the ground almost covered smooth in snow,
But a few weeds and stubble showing last.

The woods around it have it—it is theirs.   5
All animals are smothered in their lairs.
I am too absent-spirited to count;
The loneliness includes me unawares.

And lonely as it is that loneliness
Will be more lonely ere it will be less—   10
A blanker whiteness of benighted snow
With no expression, nothing to express.

They cannot scare me with their empty spaces
Between stars—on stars where no human race is.
I have it in me so much nearer home   15
To scare myself with my own desert places.

Design

(1936)

I found a dimpled spider, fat and white,
On a white heal-all, holding up a moth
Like a white piece of rigid satin cloth—
Assorted characters of death and blight
Mixed ready to begin the morning right,   5
Like the ingredients of a witches' broth—
A snow-drop spider, a flower like a froth,
And dead wings carried like a paper kite.

What had that flower to do with being white,
The wayside blue and innocent heal-all?   10
What brought the kindred spider to that height,
Then steered the white moth thither in the night?
What but design of darkness to appall?—
If design govern in a thing so small.

The Gift Outright

(1942)

The land was ours before we were the land's.
She was our land more than a hundred years
Before we were her people. She was ours
In Massachusetts, in Virginia,
But we were England's, still colonials,   5
Possessing what we still were unpossessed by,
Possessed by what we now no more possessed.
Something we were withholding made us weak
Until we found out that it was ourselves
We were withholding from our land of living,   10
And forthwith found salvation in surrender.
Such as we were we gave ourselves outright
(The deed of gift was many deeds of war)
To the land vaguely realizing westward,
But still unstoried, artless, unenhanced,   15
Such as she was, such as she would become.

DISCUSSION QUESTIONS

1. Frost's "Mending Wall" provides a good starting point for examination of his practices as a poet. Could the poem be described as a dramatic monologue? If so, who is the speaker, and to whom is he speaking? Is the poem structured as an exchange of comments between two people? What are they talking about? Provide specific evidence from "Mending Wall" to support your claims.

2. In "Mending Wall," "After Apple-Picking," and "Birches," Frost describes events observed in nature: the shifting of a stone wall after frozen ground thaws, the ripening of fruit on an apple tree, and the bending of birch trees by winter ice. Frost offers two or more possible explanations for each effect he describes. Do you see these explanations as literal or figurative? Why do Frost's speakers give the explanations they do?

3. Often Frost ends his poems with a striking statement that seems to resemble a riddle. For example, the last lines of "After Apple-Picking" refer to a woodchuck the question of whether the speaker's sleepiness is "like his / Long sleep, as I describe its coming on, / Or just some human sleep" (40–42). What does this play on the word "sleep" signify in the poem? Is Frost using irony? What does Frost do in other poems that seems similar?

4. Look at the images Frost uses in "Design," and consider the possibility that the poem is ironic. Do you see verbal irony or situational irony in Frost's choice of moth, flower, and spider—all white in this case? And what do you make of the final lines of the poem, which question the possibility of design or pattern at work in the events described?

5. How would you characterize Robert Frost's attitude toward America and its history in "The Gift Outright?" Does the poem connect, in subject or theme, to others by him? Why do you think he was asked to read this poem at President Kennedy's inauguration?

6. While Frost's poems are interesting because of what they have to say about being a human being, even about being an American, he should also be recognized as a master of poetic technique and tone. After reading several of Frost's poems aloud, can you start to describe the reasons this is the case? Does marking particular poems for rhythm help you explain the effects he can achieve?

7. Which of Frost's poems in this Casebook is your favorite? Why? Is it the persona in the poem or its subject matter that has attracted you? Is it a personal connection between the poem and yourself that draws you to it? What does this particular poem mean to you?

RESEARCH TOPICS

1. As Robert Frost himself indicates—in essays reprinted as part of this Casebook, for example—he thought long and hard about the nature of poetry and its function in society. Look at other essays and at the interviews collected in Edward Connery Lathem's *Interviews with Robert Frost*. Were his statements about poetry and about society consistent throughout his career as a writer? Or can you see him taking different positions in the 1920s and 1930s and in the 1950s?

2. The poet William Meredith begins his poem "In Memory of Robert Frost" with the lines "Everybody had to know something, and what they said /About that, the thing they'd learned by curious heart, / They said well. / That was what he wanted to hear" (1–4). Does this seem to you an accurate description of the Frost you know from reading his poems? (Look at Leslie Lee Francis's *The Frost Family's Adventure in Poetry* to see his granddaughter's recollections of the poet.) What interested him about other people and the world in which he lived? How do the poems themselves provide evidence of this?

3. Throughout the early part of Frost's career, his work was frequently compared to that of Carl Sandburg and Edwin Arlington Robinson. Find a collection of poems by one of these men and compare his work to Frost's. (The poet's essays and letters contain comments by Frost on each of his fellow poets, and you may find them helpful. Jay Parini's *Robert Frost: A Life* may also be a useful source.)

4. Frost's career as a published writer began as a result of help from a fellow expatriate, American poet Ezra Pound. While Frost was in England, he also met T. S. Eliot. Both Pound and Eliot are central figures in the development of modernist poetry, but Frost does not write like them. In fact, his attitudes toward the two remained ambivalent throughout his career. Consult Richard Poirier's *Robert Frost: The Work of Knowing* to get an overview of Frost's relationships with Eliot and Pound. Then, after formulating a working definition of literary modernism, try to figure out why Frost resisted writing like his compatriots. What was it about modernism that he disliked?

5. Eric Link's article, "Nature's Extra-Vagrants: Frost and Thoreau in the Maine Woods" (see Bibliography for complete information), argues for a connection between Frost's writing on nature and Henry David Thoreau's. Consider the possible connections between Frost and the nineteenth-century American writers Ralph Waldo Emerson and Thoreau. You might want to look at Emerson's essay "Nature" (1836) as part of your research, and you might also want to read some brief selections by Thoreau, perhaps the ones to which Link refers. Is there something particularly American about Frost's interest in nature as a subject?

6. Part of Frost's success as a poet came from the fact he made strong, positive impressions on those who heard him speak or read his poetry aloud. If you look at the Robert Frost section of the online Academy of American Poets at <http://www.poetry.org/poets>, you will find links to audio and video records of Frost's speeches and public readings. After listening to some of these recordings, consider to what extent, if any, his reputation derives from his ability to "sell" his work to people beyond the traditional world of literature.

Secondary Sources

The Figure a Poem Makes

Abstraction is an old story with the philosophers, but it has been like a new toy in the hands of the artists of our day. Why can't we have any one quality of poetry we choose by itself? We can have in thought. Then it will go hard if we can't in practice. Our lives for it.

Granted no one but the humanist much cares how sound a poem is if it is only *a* sound. The sound is the gold on the ore. Then we will have the sound out alone and dispense with the inessential. We do till we make the discovery that the object in writing poetry is to make all poems sound as different as possible from each other, and the resources for that of vowels, consonants, punctuation, syntax, words, sentences, meter are not enough. We need the help of context—meaning—subject matter. That is the greatest help towards variety. All that can be done with words is soon told. So also with meters—particularly in our language where there are virtually but two, strict iambic and loose iambic. The ancients with many were still poor if they depended on meters for all tune. It is painful to watch our sprung-rhythmists straining at the point of omitting one short from a foot for relief from monotony. The possibilities for tune from the dramatic tones of meaning struck across the rigidity of a limited meter are endless. And we are back in poetry as merely one more art of having something to say, sound or unsound. Probably better if sound, because deeper and from wider experience.

Then there is this wildness whereof it is spoken. Granted again that it has an equal claim with sound to being a poem's better half. If it is a wild tune, it is a poem. Our problem then is, as modern abstractionists, to have the wildness pure; to be wild with nothing to be wild about. We bring up as aberrationists, giving way to undirected associations and kicking ourselves from one chance suggestion to another in all directions as of a hot afternoon in the life of a grasshopper. Theme alone can steady us down. Just as the first mystery was how a poem could have a tune in such a straightness as meter, so the second mystery is how a poem can have wildness and at the same time a subject that shall be fulfilled.

It should be of the pleasure of a poem itself to tell how it can. The figure a poem makes. It begins in delight and ends in wisdom. The figure is the same as for love. No one can really hold that the ecstasy should be static and stand still in one place. It begins in delight, it inclines to the impulse, it assumes direction with the first line laid down, it runs a course of lucky events, and ends in a clarification of life—not necessarily a great clarification, such as sects and cults are founded on, but in a momentary stay against confusion. It has denouement. It has an outcome that though unforeseen was predestined from the first image of the original mood—and indeed from the very mood. It is but a trick poem and no poem at all if the best of it was thought of first and saved for the last. It finds its own name as it goes and discovers the best waiting for it in some final phrase at once wise and sad—the happy-sad blend of the drinking song.

No tears in the writer, no tears in the reader. No surprise for the writer, no surprise for the reader. For me the initial delight is in the surprise of remembering something I didn't know I knew. I am in a place, in a situation, as if I had materialized from cloud or risen out of the ground. There is a glad recognition of the long lost and the rest follows. Step by step the wonder of unexpected supply keeps growing. The impressions most useful to my purpose seem always those I was unaware of and so made no note of at the time when taken, and the conclusion is come to that like giants we are always hurling experience ahead of us to pave the future with against the day when we may want to strike a line of purpose across it for somewhere. The line will have the more charm for not being mechanically straight. We enjoy the straight crookedness of a good walking stick. Modern instruments of precision are being used to make things crooked as if by eye and hand in the old days.

I tell how there may be a better wildness of logic than of inconsequence. But the logic is backward, in retrospect, after the act. It must be more felt than seen ahead like prophecy. It must be a revelation, or a series of revelations, as much for the poet as for the reader. For it to be that there must have been the greatest freedom of the material to move about in it and to establish relations in it regardless of time and space, previous relation, and everything but affinity. We prate of freedom. We call our schools free because we are not free to stay away from them till we are sixteen years of age. I have given up my democratic prejudices and now willingly set the lower classes free to be completely taken care of by the upper classes. Political freedom is nothing to me. I bestow it right and left. All I would keep for myself is the freedom of my material—the condition of body and mind now and then to summons aptly from the vast chaos of all I have lived through.

Scholars and artists thrown together are often annoyed at the puzzle of where they differ. Both work for knowledge; but I suspect they differ most importantly in the way their knowledge is come by. Scholars get theirs with conscientious thoroughness along projected lines of logic; poets theirs cavalierly and as it happens in and out of books. They stick to nothing deliberately, but let what will stick to them like burrs where they walk in the field. No acquirement is on assignment, or even self-assignment. Knowledge of the second kind is much more available in the wild free ways of wit and art. A school boy may be defined as one who can tell you what he knows in the order in which he learned it. The artist must value himself as he snatches a thing from some previous order in time and space into a new order with not so much as a ligature clinging to it of the old place where it was organic.

More than once I should have lost my soul to radicalism if it had been the originality it was mistaken for by its young converts. Originality and initiative are what I ask for my country. For myself the originality need be no more than the freshness of a poem run in the way I have described: from delight to wisdom. The figure is the same as for love. Like a piece of ice on a hot stove the poem must ride on its own melting. A poem may be worked over once it is in being, but may not be worried into being. Its most precious quality will remain its having run itself and carried away the poet with it. Read it a hundred times: it will forever keep its freshness as a metal keeps its fragrance. It can never lose its sense of a meaning that once unfolded by surprise as it went.

ROBERT FROST

Poetry and School

Why poetry is in school more than it seems to be outside in the word, the children haven't been told. They must wonder.

The authorities that keep poetry in school may be divided into two kinds, those with a conscientious concern for it and those with a real weakness for it. They are easily told apart.

School is founded on the invention of letters and numbers. The inscription over every school door should be the rhyme A B C and One Two Three. The rest of education is apprenticeship and for me doesn't belong in school.

The chief reason for going to school is to get the impression fixed for life that there is a book side to everything.

We go to college to be given one more chance to learn to read in case we haven't learned in High School. Once we have learned to read the rest can be trusted to add itself unto us.

The way to read a poem in prose or verse is in the light of all the other poems ever written. We may begin anywhere. We *duff* into our first. We read that imperfectly (thoroughness with it would be fatal), but the better to read the second. We read the second the better to read the third, the third the better to read the fourth, the fourth the better to read the fifth, the fifth the better to read the first again, or the second if it so happens. For poems are not meant to be read in course any more than they are to be made a study of. I once made a resolve never to put any book to any use it wasn't intended for by its author. Improvement will not be a progression but a widening circulation. Our instinct is to settle down like a revolving dog and make ourselves at home among the poems, completely at our ease as to how they should be taken. The same people will be apt to take poems right as know how to take a hint when there is one and not to take a hint when none is intended. Theirs is the ultimate refinement.

We write in school chiefly because to try our hand at writing should make us better readers.

Almost everyone should almost have experienced the fact that a poem is an idea caught fresh in the act of dawning.

Also that felicity can't be fussed into existence.

Also that there is such a thing as having a moment. And that the great thing is to know a moment when you have one.

Also to know what Catullus means by *mens animi.*

Also to know that poetry and prose too regarded as poetry is the renewal of words.

Emotion removes a word from its base for the moment by metaphor, but often in the long run even on to a new base. The institution, the form, the word, have regularly or irregularly to be renewed from the root of the spirit. That is the creed of the true radical

Emotions must be dammed back and harnessed by discipline to the wit mill, not just turned loose in exclamations. No force will express far that isn't shut in by discipline at all the pores to jet at one outlet only. Emotion has been known to ooze off.

Better readers, yes, and better writers too, if possible. Certainly not worse writers as many are made by being kept forever at it with the language (not to say jargon) of criticism and appreciation. The evil days will come soon enough, and we shall have no pleasure in them, when we shall have dried up into nothing but abstractions. The best educated person is one who has been matured at just the proper rate. Seasoned but not kiln dried. The starch thickening has to be stirred in with slow care. The arteries will harden fast enough without being helped. Too many recent poems have been actually done in the language of evaluation. They are too critical in spirit to admit of further criticism.

And this constant saying what amounts to no more than variations on the theme of "I don't like this and I do like that" tends to aesthetic Puritanism. "For goodness' sake," said one teacher to a class, "write for a change about what you are neither for nor against." When one bold boy asked if there could be any such thing, he was told he had flunked the course.

The escape is to action in words: to stories, plays, scenes, episodes, and incidents.

Practice of an art is more salutary than talk about it. There is nothing more composing than composition.

We were enjoined of old to learn to write now while young so that if we ever had anything to say later we would know how to say it. All there is to learning to write or talk is learning how to have something to say.

Our object is to say something that *is* something. One teacher once said that it was something at once valid and sensational with the accent on both. Classmates punish us for failure better than the teachers by very dead silence or exchanging glances at our expense.

One of the dangers of college to anyone who wants to stay a human reader (that is to say a humanist) is that he will become a specialist and lose his sensitive fear of landing on the lovely too hard. (With beak and talon.)

Another danger nowadays to sensitiveness is getting inured to translations. The rarity of a poem well brought over from one language into another should be a warning. Some translation of course in course for utility. But never enough to get broken to it. For self assurance there should always be a lingering unhappiness in reading translations.

The last place along the line where books are safely read as they are going to be out in the world in polite society is usually in so-called Freshman English. There pupils are still treated as if not all of them were going to turn out scholars.

The best reader of all is one who will read, can read, no faster than he can hear the lines and sentences in his mind's ear as if aloud. Frequenting poetry has slowed him down by its metric or measured pace.

The eye reader is a barbarian. So also is the writer for the eye reader, who needn't care how badly he writes since he doesn't care how badly he is read.

It is one thing to think the text and be totally absorbed in it. There is however an ascendancy in the mood to spare that can also think ABOUT the text. From the induced parallel current in the mind over and above the text the notes are drawn that we so much resent other people's giving us because we want the fun of having them for ourselves.

A B C is letters. One Two Three is numbers—mathematica. What marks verse off from prose is that it talks in numbers. Numbers is the nickname for poetry. Poetry plays the rhythms of dramatic speech on the grid of meter. A good map carries its own scale of miles.

For my pleasure I had soon write free verse as play tennis with the net down.

MILTON BRACKER

He Himself Is Perhaps the Biggest Metaphor of All

Robert Frost is a poet whose work and personal appearances have moved thousands of Americans to a demonstrativeness that might easily be associated with the presence of a heroic athlete or a movie star. When he says his poems (the verb he insists on—he never "reads" them), it is to standing-room-only audiences. And the response is based not on superficial idolatry but on a deep-set and affectionate admiration often bordering on awe.

At eighty-four, Robert Frost has won four Pulitzer Prizes and been cited by more institutions of higher learning than there are in any college football conference. He has jested that he would rather get a degree than an education; but this is simply to be gracious to the donors. Actually, he has not only had an education of his own (though never a baccalaureate degree), but as a teacher, both fixed and itinerant, has contributed preferred shares of stock to the educational portfolios held by several generations of scholars.

But the impact of Robert Frost on poetry and on those who love it is possibly less than his impact as a personality on anyone who gets near him. If you have had considerable experience in "interviewing" people, you are still not prepared for this white-haired New Englander (who, improbably, was born in San Francisco), because he is like no statesman, celebrity, or ordinary human being you have ever interviewed. Robert Frost, newly honored by appointment as poetry consultant to the Library of Congress, is quietly but unmistakably overwhelming.

"There's nothing in me to be afraid of," he will assure you. "I'm too off-hand; I'm an offhander."

But there is a deadly joke in his offhandedness. As he says, slipping it in casually, in another connection, "I bear watching." Moreover, he will let you know disarmingly that, "I'm not confused; I'm only well-mixed." And he might have added of himself, as he frequently remarks of certain of his most-quoted and picked-apart poems, that he is "loaded with ulteriority."

"You have to look out for everybody's metaphors," says Robert Frost. He himself is perhaps the biggest metaphor of all. He even *looks* like a symbol.

His hair is really white and really silky; a mass of it tends to sift down to the left side of his forehead like snow to one corner of a window. His eyes are pale blue, cragged by heavy brows with white curls wintering them. His lower lip is the thicker; it juts a little. In the over-all he is massive, often understandably likened to rough-hewn granite.

He had an "altercation with a surgeon"—there is a virtually imperceptible scar on his right cheek. But the real scar is the scar of living, and no man ever wore it more proudly or with more stunning effect, as photographers have discovered.

Even in the impersonal formality of a New York hotel room, he would prefer to be tieless. He wears high black shoes and is apt to leave them half unlaced. His hands show virtually no spots of age. His grip is firm and wholly unself-conscious. And when he walks down an aisle to a stage or platform, he strides strongly and directly, as completely in command of the situation as of the loyalty and awe of those in the audience. His voice is resonant to the level of being gravelly; he may use it to repeat things he has said many times before. But he is psychologically incapable of speaking a cliché or of arranging words in a commonplace manner.

Still, an interview has to have a "plan of campaign," Robert Frost acknowledged. So what more natural than a little starter about his new job? He seized upon the word "consultant" in his new title.

"As the greatest living authority on education," he began, with a twinkle. "I particularly want to be consulted by the foundations."

Robert Frost has had one publisher for forty-three years. His books have sold more than four hundred thousand copies, and he has actually made a living out of poetry, although he once had to give up buying a painting he wanted because he could not get it for one thousand dollars. But the implication was clear: If, through his new post, he could interest those who might assist other poets, he was eager to do so.

He passed a hand over his face and injected a mild qualification, "I'm not to advocate anything," he said. "I can describe better than I can advocate. I'm a reporter; you should have seen me at Rutgers. . . ."

He was referring to an occasion where—as at the New School for Social Research a few nights later—poetry, as personified by Robert Frost, "gets mobbed."

But (with no specific reference to either audience) Robert Frost, the reporter, was not to be taken in by the externals.

"You want to watch for those people who seem to enjoy what they don't understand," he said. The "partisans" of Ezra Pound, for example, and "I can't be called that."[. . .]

"You can't make a poem without a point."

He laughed, remembering having said it another way: "You've got to snap the quip to make Pegasus prance."

Robert Frost is much too human not to be pleased by his own phrase-making.

"Snap the quip," he repeated, with a chuckle. "I could make up a joke at a banquet, use it in a different way at another banquet. I'm very instructive; I'm very accidental. I go barding around, and all that. Barding around."

He frequently "bards around" with college presidents and has warm regard and great respect for several.

"But I'm aware that some of them have no interest in it, and that's all right," he said.

Again the raised brows, the fleeting laugh that lights up the weathered face like a sudden shaft of sunlight.

"They *have* to be present when they decorate me," he added. Then more seriously, "I'm not as anxious about poetry as I am about these poor college presidents."

Apart from the problems faced by the educators, there was a criterion he liked to apply: "He's on our side." He mentioned four of whom that might be said, then fretted a little lest he had left out some others. He is always elliptical in his language; never in his sense of friendship.

Robert Frost has defined poetry as "that which is lost from prose and verse in translation." As for the great poets, Shakespeare "knew more about psychiatry and people like Othello and Desdemona" than any twenty-five-dollar-an-hour man.

Robert Frost considered the Moor for a moment as an analyst's patient.

"The psychiatrist would advise him not to smother her," he decided.

Then his quick eyes changed reflectively.

"But some of them are awful good at it," he admitted.

He was reminded of his own insights—his incredible exactness with words, as when, in "Blue-Butterfly Day," he wrote of the wheels that "freshly sliced the April mire," thus choosing the absolutely correct verb, the one so uniquely evocative as to renew and fix many readers the experience of observing such a wheel in such mud for all time. And the other exactnesses: the swimming buck pushing the *crumpled* water; the ice crystals from the birch branch *avalanching* on the snow crust.

Robert Frost's browned face crinkled at the references.

"That's what I live for," he said—the appreciation, in detail, of the essential purity of his work. "It cuts a little edge across your feelings," he said.

Then he talked of the American attitude toward poetry, of the time he and a distinguished scientist met and he had begun, "Let's you and I compare science and poetry; that's what I live for."

The other said, "You mean the exactness of science and the inexactness of poetry?"

" 'Oh,' I said," said Robert Frost, " 'you mean poetry is inexact. If you mean that, I'm going home.' "

"He said, 'Let's change the subject.' "

And he told of the diplomat who had spent a lot on modern art and liked to be regarded as something of an expert on it, but who remarked of a young relative with poetic inclinations, "We hoped he'd get over it." Robert Frost had not enjoyed that.

On the other hand, he know businessmen who really had "the same gentle weakness for the arts."

"A man will say, 'I'm just an engineer,' " he went on, "yet he will read more poetry than anyone I know."

And he linked this to the "greatest triumph in life; that's what everything turns on: to be reminded of something you hardly knew you knew." He said it gave you the feeling, "Oh, what a good boy am I."

Then, inevitably, I brought up "Stopping by Woods on a Snowy Evening." He had "said" this a few nights before at the New School, pronouncing it a little rapidly—a little too rapidly to permit the emotion of those in the audience (who had been gripped by it for anywhere from thirty minutes to thirty years) to break out in applause. There is of course a growing literature about these sixteen lines; and Robert Frost took it in stride.

"Now, that's all right," he said; "it's out of my hands once it's published." His protagonist might have said:

But I have promises to keep,
And miles to go before I sleep . . .

simply because he was having a pleasant social evening, and it was time to go home. Yet Robert Frost knew it had often been taken as a "death poem."

"I never intended that," he said, "but I did have the feeling it was loaded with ulteriority." He said it was written one night back in the Twenties, when he was a "little excited from getting over-tired—they call it autointoxicated."

In the stanza he made what he called an "unnecessary commitment"— the line

My little horse must think it queer

But he rode it out; he "triumphed over it."

And, he went on, there was "that thing about every poem. I didn't see the end until I got to it. Every poem is a voyage of discovery. I go in to see if I can get out, like you go to the North Pole. Once you've said the first line, the rest of it's got to be."

Robert Frost leaned heavily toward his visitor, as on a rostrum he seems to move gradually closer to each individual in the hall.

"The glory of any particular poem," he continued, "is once you've tasted that arrival at the end. That what makes all the difference."

But in poetry, as in other struggles, the defeats need not be "inglorious." Again, as always, with Robert Frost, it was doing what had to be done and doing it bravely. It was triumph of spirit over matter. It was people "not believing, and then having to believe."

Robert Frost has one "ruthless purpose" and that is poetry. But he is as aware of the police story on page one of the morning paper as of the so-called advent of the space age. He take it all in perspective.

He was at Kitty Hawk in 1893, before the Wright Brothers. Some time after their historic flight he wrote a poem called "Kitty Hawk." Thus, early aeronautics and recent rocketry are in a sense the same to him; they are both part of the "great enterprise of the spirit into matter." Science is the great "lock-picker." Science goes "on, on, on; but the wonder of philosophy is that it stops."

Since man knew all along that the moon and the planets were there, it was inevitable that scientists would be "risking spirit" to get there. And that poets would write of where they were trying to get, and why.

As for Robert Frost himself:

"About one-tenth of my poems are astronomical; and I've had a glass a good deal of the time." (He meant a telescope but, as in so many things he says, the figurative interpretation was at least as accurate.)

He said the young missile men were doing a "fine, daring, bold thing." They were sharing the "great event of history"—science. And science meant the "dash of the spirit into the material," no matter how remote.

But Robert Frost has always had his feet on the earth, too. And as for the two powers that seemed in contention for this planet (as well as in a race to the moon), he saw their opposed systems as evidencing "two great ideas—who's to say they're not both valid?"

"I don't look to the time when they're going to throw away their dream of Utopia," he said, without naming the Russians.[. . .]

Robert Frost had not read Boris Pasternak; he preferred not to discuss the case of the Soviet Nobel Prize winner as an individual. But in general terms:

"What they're ridiculing him for is from selfishness. They don't want their own thing reflected on—it's treason. We stand all that better than they do."

He glanced back to 1954 and the late Senator Joseph R. McCarthy, and resumed:

"We do stand it perfectly. Poor McCarthy. He seems to me like a soldier boy who couldn't bear to hear parlor pinks sitting around and talking the way they did. . . .

"Our freedom allows us great extremes of thought, and we almost let our people plot against us. But I don't see how you can help doing something for your own existence. All you have to do in court is prove the other fellow was about to shoot you. You can have a pretty good time in court if you can prove that."

The conversation narrowed back to Robert Frost himself. He spoke of sleep.

"Just as I feel I never have to go to sleep," he said, "little dreams begin to come over me—voices, sometimes—and I know I am gone. There is a curious connection between reverie, meditation, and dreams."

The very night before, he had dreamed of stumbling and falling. And often he would dream of a boyhood experience when, mistaken in thinking "I bore a charmed life," he got a "terrible dose of hornets." Now he dreams of the hornets, yet never so deeply as to be unaware of his actual situation. "I'm aware of the blankets," he said, a little wonderingly. Safe in bed, he pulls them up over his head and thwarts the dream-swarm.

He said a magazine has recently listed him as "one of the oldest living men."

"Funny, isn't it, about living on?" he mused. "They didn't educate me when I was young—the doctor said I was delicate and wouldn't live long. That's probably what prolongs life."

He went further in paradox.

"I'm not the kind of man who thinks the world can be saved by knowledge. It can only be saved by daring, bravery, going ahead. . . ."

"I have done many things that it looked as if it was impossible to do—like going on the platform. I did it because I didn't have to face bullets."

He said he wondered what it must be like to stand before a firing squad.

I told him I had seen a German general face one in Italy in December, 1945.

"Did he do it bravely?" Robert Frost asked.

I told him he had done it very bravely.

There was a television set in the corner, and it seemed reasonable to ask if he took any interest in the medium.

"I do a little of it," he said, meaning being viewed, rather than viewing. "It's so when I see Peter at the gate, and he says, 'Have you lived modern?' I can say 'I've flown and I've been on TV.' "

How about the Beat Generation?

"They're not even beat," said Robert Frost.

JOHN J. CONDER

"After Apple-Picking": Frost's Troubled Sleep

"What do I want to communicate but what a *hell* of a good time I had writing it?" Frost once asked. He hastened to explain what he meant by the "good time" he had when writing a poem. "The whole thing is performance and prowess and feats of association. Why don't critics talk about those things—what a feat it was to turn that that way, and what a feat it was to remember that, to be reminded of that by this? Why don't they talk about that?"[1] Frost's mild impatience with critics clearly implies that his poems are ordered, even though the world of nature appearing in them may resist man's attempts to order it. The problem is that critics, having recognized the depth of the actual in Frost's poetry, have had difficulty unravelling all the strands of the associative pattern operating in certain poems. And in the very attempt to show that the literal meaning of such poems is far from the full meaning, they have limited the poems in other ways.

"After Apple-Picking" is such a poem. A work which one critic describes as "absorbed with 'states-between' "[2] necessarily attracts the same kind of attention given to an evocative poem like Coleridge's "Kubla Khan." And the commentaries clearly illustrate the problem of tracking down Frost's associations. The poem contains a dream, and dreams easily evoke associations with the ideal. This is the association made by the most familiar reading, according to which the poem shows that the ideal "is to be understood as a projection, a development, of the literal experience."[3] The poem also contains apples, and an apple is easily associated with the religious doctrine of the Fall. A more recent interpretation explores this possibility, calling "After Apple-Picking" "a witty, blasphemous poem" which rejects Christian doctrine.[4] The first reading tries to be flexible, allowing for many applications of the theme; the second does not. Together the two interpretations raise the question which is crucial for so many of Frost's poems: What framework should be applied to guide the critic in determining the associations which are operative?

Clearly each element of the poem must be examined in its complex relationship to all the others; but to minimize the danger of subjective interpretations unintended by the poet, these relationships must be modified by an understanding of Frost's world. Frost, of course, has not left us his *Vision*, but other poems of his can illuminate his intention, and critical analyses of his world provide some help. So do scattered comments made by Frost himself, one of the most important of which states that he has a habit or "talking contraries" and hence in any given poem "could unsay everything . . . [he] said, nearly."[5]

Approaching "After Apple-Picking" with an eye for contraries unravels many of the puzzles in the poem and reveals its richness. The central problems of the poem are posed in the opening lines of its conclusion with the introduction of the ambiguous word "trouble" and the provocative image of "sleep": "One can see what will trouble / This sleep of mine, whatever sleep it is." Although the trouble and the "sleep" are intimately connected in the lines, for purposes of analysis it is best to keep them separate. The speaker himself does so, since he apparently knows what will trouble his sleep but is uncertain about the kind of sleep overtaking him. Arranged in the order most convenient for answering them, two

questions emerge in "After Apple-Picking": What is the nature of the
sleep? What is the nature of the trouble?

′ A complex of familiar references points to death as one possible form
of sleep. The very situation of the poem, a surcease from picking apples,
recalls the Garden of Eden from which, after the apple was picked (and
eaten), man was expelled into a world of sin and death. The speaker
affirms that he was "well" on his way to sleep even before his morning
venture with the sheet of ice. Since life is a process ending in death, the
speaker's comment, juxtaposed against the reference to "heaven," pro-
motes the possibility that the speaker may be journeying to an immortal
sleep. The season of the year emphasizes nature's death, while the woodchuck's hibernation suggests a pattern of death and resurrection.

Intriguing though these references are, a reader familiar with Frost's
playful ways ("I like to fool," he said)[6] knows better than to take them
hastily at face value. The most popular reading rejects the possibility of
death. Since the speaker's dream, according to this account, represents an
ideal rooted in the real world, his ability to dream about a job well done
represents his heaven on earth. His capacity for contemplation sets him
apart from the inferior woodchuck, though he does not affirm that man
has an immortal soul.[7]

Insofar as this reading rejects death and immortality as one possible
form of sleep in "After Apple-Picking," the commentary is consistent with
a general opinion that Frost is nonteleological in his thought. Since he
neither affirms nor denies that the emergence of mind suggests ultimate
meaning in the universe,[8] Frost would necessarily remain neutral in his
attitude toward immortality. But if the speaker's dream and sleep exist in
life, then to assert that, after his labors, the speaker "is now looking not
into the world of effort but the world of dream, of the renewal,"[9] is to over-
simplify the poem. This view identifies the dream (interpreted as plea-
surable) with the sleep (seen as a time for contemplation as well as
renewal) and in the process limits both. Such a reading qualifies the word
"trouble" into insignificance (to be troubled by a lovely dream is to be
superior to the woodchuck, who cannot dream) and oversimplifies the
speaker's attitude toward his experience. Given the feats of association
that he makes, given the fact that he speaks in contraries, the speaker's
attitude toward his sleep is far more complicated than at first seems
clear, and his trouble far more real than might be supposed.

The speaker's attitude toward his sleep is complicated because of the
possible kinds of sleep overtaking him. To be sure, this may be a night's

sleep from which the speaker will awake, refreshed, ready to turn to those "fresh tasks" mentioned by the puzzled speaker of "The Wood-Pile." This possibility is supported by the reference to "night"; it is at "night" that he is "drowsing off"; the speaker, having completed the last of his labors as best he could, may be about to got to bed.

But the association of night with "essence of winter sleep" gives "night" a metaphoric context and so expands its meaning. Indeed, a simple night's sleep seems an improbable meaning, since the speaker was "well" upon his way to sleep before he dropped the "pane of glass" in the morning. Perhaps, then, his drowsy state may be part of the "essence of winter sleep"; that is, perhaps it is a sleep similar to nature's. Enough correspondences between the human and natural worlds exist to dictate this as one possible kind of sleep. The speaker's apple-picking ceases as the year nears conclusion, and his "drowsing off" is associated with "essence of winter sleep":

> Essence of winter sleep is on the night,
> The scent of apples: I am drowsing off.

If his sleep is to be like nature's, what then is the point of the reference to the woodchuck? Since the woodchuck surely could *not* ". . . say whether it's like his / Long sleep, as I describe its coming on, / Or just some human sleep," the speaker's avowal to the contrary apparently reduces the conclusion to mere whimsy. Presumably woodchucks do not dream and do not desire great harvests. Men do. Presumably men do not go into physical hibernation for months. Woodchucks do. But the point of the reference to the woodchuck is not simply to create a contrast between a human and an animal sleep but also to introduce an implied comparison—an inexact analogy between the speaker's sleep and the sleep of nature.[10] If only man has the potential to desire great harvests, his desires may follow a cycle similar to nature's. They may wax and wane like (or with) the seasons; they may emerge, as the woodchuck does in the spring, or lie dormant for months, as the woodchuck does in winter.

For the man who is ". . . overtired / Of the great harvest I myself desired," such an analogy carries with it its own measure or reassurance. Assuming that the desire for harvests and the act of harvesting together are an emblem of man's creative spirit working its will on the world, a reader can see that implicit in this situation is the question: Will my desire, my will, my talents be resurrected, directed toward reaping new harvests? Although he would find it more comforting to think that "just some human sleep" is a single night's sleep which will restore his powers so that he can turn to "fresh tasks," he can be reassured by the analogy between man and the seasons nonetheless. His desires will lie dormant longer, but they will surely be revived, as nature is. In this case, the speaker will be in the happy position of his counterpart in an earlier work, "To the Thawing Wind," a poem employing many of the same images as "After Apple-Picking." Concerned only with drawing a direct parallel between himself and nature, the speaker of the earlier poem implores the wind: "Give the buried flower a dream." Entreating it further ("Bathe my window, make it flow, / Melt it as the ice will go"), he concludes:

> Scatter poems on the floor;
> Turn the poet out of door.

But "After Apple-Picking" has considerably more depth than "To the Thawing Wind," and the analogy between man and nature, which reassures that man's creative life has wellsprings much like nature's or is as automatic in its processes as those of nature, does not quite hold. The speaker himself is uncertain of the analogy, speculating whether his sleep is like the woodchuck's, ". . . *as I describe its coming on*, / Or just some human sleep" (italics mine). As he has described that sleep coming on, indeed, the speaker clearly has been speaking contraries. The analogy with nature which his associations establish are, in the process of his speaking, undermined by suggestions that the sleep will be different from nature's.

Those suggestions become explicit in the contrast between the sleep of the woodchuck and "just some human sleep." Precisely because the implied comparison between the speaker's sleep and the woodchuck's is undone by the power of the contrast (men *can* only have a human sleep), the assurance offered by the comparison with nature is also retracted. The contrast between the two kinds of sleep, furthermore, has been anticipated from the beginning of the poem, thus providing the fullest impact to the concluding line, "Or just some human sleep."

From the outset, nature seems to have become alien to the speaker. The first section concludes with the speaker's commenting that he is no longer interested in picking apples, in appropriating nature to his own uses: "But I am done with apple-picking now." The parallel between his drowsiness and the "essence of winter sleep" is, at best, tenuous, held together by an uncommitted colon in the last line of the statement, "Essence of winter sleep is on the night, / The scent of apples: I am drowsing off." The "essence," in short, is more directly associated with the "scent of apples" than with the speaker's sleep. The parallel tenuously established by the colon breaks down in the next section, which describes the strange sight of the winter world through a sheet of ice. Perhaps he does see through this "glass" "the world of hoary grass," but even that is not certain, and no other object in the external world he views is mentioned. Before he describes the "form" of his dreaming, he significantly lets the pane of ice fall and break, an action in stark contrast to his behavior during the harvest, when he took special pains to keep the apples from falling. Of course, since the ice is melting, the gesture is perfectly normal. Deliberate mention of the detail, nonetheless, suggests his alienation from nature. Once he could handle it (in the literal and metaphoric senses of that term); now he cannot.

If the speaker is divorced from nature, then what would "just some human sleep" be? One can concede that the speaker is physically and mentally fatigued, his desire for a "great harvest" satiated. In that case it is *possible* that he is entering the world of renewal, that his sleep will be composed of pleasant dreams, a contemplation of the ideal based on the real; and it is *possible* that his trouble will be minimal, composed of the physical aftereffects of too much apple-picking: the "ache" and the "pressure" retained by his "instep arch"; the feel of the swaying ladder; the "rumbling sound" of the apples. But it is not at all *certain* that his is the sleep of renewal. Indeed, to argue with certainty that this is the sleep of renewal, a reader would have to rest his case on the analogy between man's cycle and nature's, an analogy that seems to fail in the poem. Such an analogy, furthermore, would not be consistent with Frost's point of view, one which sharply differentiates man from nature. A previous critic has argued persuasively that Frost believes, with Emerson, "that nature can be used to uncover and illustrate the underlying laws of the universe, because it operates by such laws. . . . Frost does not take Emerson's next step, to insist that the laws of outer nature correspond to the laws of inner mind."[11] Both Frost's habit of speaking contraries and his point of view toward nature militate against a simplistic view of sleep and argue for a darker side of "just some human sleep."

That darker side can be discerned by recalling what is lost by the failure of the analogy between man and nature. If nature can renew itself automatically, man, viewed as distinct from nature, cannot be assured of such renewal. Nature has her unknown source of creative revival. What is man's? The source of his creativity is the assumption that his harvest has value, that the activity is worthwhile. If the speaker questions the purpose of his activity, doubts the value of his harvest, then indeed his may be a sleep of the creative powers, one which will last until the doubts are removed.

The speaker makes it eminently clear that he once highly valued his harvest. Simply put, he "desired" a "great harvest," and the desire was sufficiently strong to justify extraordinary discipline and control: "There were ten thousand fruit to touch, / Cherish in hand, lift down, and not let fall." The sense of value which he associated with manual contact ("cherish in hand") is confirmed in the lines immediately following:

> For all
> That struck the earth,
> No matter if not bruised or spiked with stubble,
> Went surely to the cider-apple heap
> As of no worth.

The crucial phrase, "As of no worth," is ambiguous and reflects the speaker's habit of "talking contraries," of retracting "everything . . . [he] said, nearly." For to describe the fallen apples *as* "of no worth" is to imply their worth. It is not possible to tell whether the speaker, now commenting with the advantage of hindsight, would have characterized these apples in the same way during the actual apple-picking. What is clear is that this description of his past activities implies a sense of relative values (fallen apples are inferior to harvested ones), but a highly ambiguous one. Since the speaker has declared that ". . . I am overtired / Of the great harvest I myself desired," he is in a mood to apply the same logic of talking contraries to the harvest itself. If the fallen applies are *as* "of no worth," then, he hints, the harvest itself is *as* of great worth, a description which implies its opposite. The exhausted speaker, in short, is in doubt about his values.

Doubts related to questions of value are in his mind as he recounts his apple-picking, so it is not surprising that the dream induced by his venture reflects his confusion. It is by no means certain, of course, whether the "dreaming" is confined to the visual description of the apples or whether it includes all the aftereffects of picking apples. Since this is probably more than a simple night's sleep, it is likely that the dream is much more like one experienced when awake, as when a person still feels the rocking of the boat even after he has set foot on firm land. Assuming that the dream embraces the full range of sensations, the reader can observe a striking contrast between the visual and the other sensory elements. Only the apples are "magnified"; there is no suggestion that the "ache," the "pressure," the swaying of the ladder and the rumbling of the apples are felt and heard more intensely than during the actual pursuit of the harvest. Not only are the apples larger than life; they are also autonomous, independent of the speaker's control as they appear in the mind's eye: "Magnified apples appear and disappear."

The erratic movement of the apples, certainly, may be quite consistent with the nature of this dream, one experienced when awake. Stare at an object long enough and its impression is retained after the eyes are closed. The eyelids blink shut, and the speaker sees apples. They flick open, and the apples vanish. Quite possibly the image so retained is magnified. But for readers concerned with the depth of the actual in Frost's poetry, such an explanation is hardly sufficient. Frost no doubt wants to show that the form of the speaker's dreaming is a consequence of the activity which inspired it, since the speaker concludes the dream with the statement, "*For* I have had too much / Of apple-picking: I am overtired" (italics mine), and then describes the apple-picking itself. To settle for a purely naturalistic explanation of the relationship between the two, however, is to limit the poem.

A comparison between the dream and the activity is revealing for what the dream leaves out, and such a comparison must be based on the visual element in the dream, since all the other elements are ascribable to purely natural aftereffects and bear no symbolic relationship to the whole point of picking as many apples as possible: to reap a great harvest. The sense of discipline associated with value during the apple-picking is not present in the dream. The apples are unrelated to the speaker, moving of their own accord, without his direction, his sense of purpose. Furthermore, they are all magnified; the distinction between those harvested and those lost does not exist. Gone is the speaker's sense of relative values. Associated with the statement ". . . I am overtired / Of the great harvest I myself desired," their magnification and autonomy bring into bold relief the very doubts surfacing toward the end of his description of the actual venture of picking apples. He has literally lost sight of all the values of the harvest. If this *is* a happy sleep of contemplation, the happiness is highly qualified.

Concerned about his values, the speaker is also concerned about the nature of his sleep, a concern imaged in the contrast between himself and the woodchuck. As part of nature, the woodchuck will automatically be renewed. But the speaker may need, for renewal, not simply rest, some period of dormancy, but also some certain knowledge of human values. And where is such knowledge to come from? Recall, this is a poem about what happens *after* apple-picking. Hardly an allegory either supporting or denouncing Christian doctrine, the work nonetheless relies on over-tones of the Fall to enrich its complex meaning. When man first picked the apple, he was expelled from Eden to labor by the sweat of his brow, a consequence of his newly found knowledge of good and evil. The speaker lives in a fallen world where he has labored and sweated. But he gains no sure knowledge as Adam did. His ladder is pointed *toward* heaven only, and he has had to descend from it. Man can climb the ladder toward heaven, toward certainty, but when he returns, he discovers how little he has learned with certainty. He cannot even know the nature of his sleep, although the possibilities seem clear.

Perhaps his will be like the woodchuck's sleep, the sleep of nature, in the limited sense that his creative powers are subject to the same kind of cyclical movement observed in the seasons. At worst, this sleep would be like nature's in its duration, though not in its character (unlike nature, man can dream). Such a sleep, induced by physical and mental fatigue, is not a function of man's uncertain values. His values are certain; his abil-ity to act on them, limited. This is the sleep of renewal.

This meaning of "sleep," though possible in the poem, seems obviated by the apparent failure of the analogy between man and nature. Al-though Frost allows for its possibility in the reference to the woodchuck, such a sleep seems inconsistent with his larger view of man and nature. A second possible sleep, not far removed from the first, is also ascribable to a straining of the physical and mental powers, a strain just severe enough to confuse the speaker's sense of values and to blur his sense of purpose. But if he originally possesses a firmly grounded sense of value and purpose, he can be reasonably certain he will awaken from this sleep, from this confusion about values. A good rest, a night's or a month's, will settle the matter. Thereafter, he can turn to "fresh tasks" with no need to investigate his values. Given Frost's larger poetic world, this meaning is the most likely. The will to live and to create provides the ground for man's values.

But in the world of "After Apple-Picking," recovery is not certain. Frost's "feats of association" are so complicated, his performance in hint-ing so masterful, that the poem suggests the possibility of a third kind of sleep. If the speaker's encounter with the apples has led him to question not just the nature, but the *source* of his values, then his sleep may be longer, even permanent. It is one matter to recover values lost because of fatigue. It is another to be forced to return to their source, particularly if that source is only the "I myself" who "desired." For when desire fails and values falter, what source outside the self can restore desire? In "After Apple-Picking," the ladder only points *toward* heaven.

What *will* trouble the speaker's sleep, whatever sleep it is? He is only falling asleep in this poem, and he does not yet know which sleep his will be. Its duration will determine its nature. It is his uncertainty as to when (or whether) he will awaken which will be carried into his sleep, troubling it. Ironically enough, only when he awakens will he know what sleep it is—or, rather, was.

NOTES*

1. Tape-recorded interview with Robert Frost. From *Writers at Work: The Paris Review Interviews*, Second Series, (New York: Viking Press, 1963), 32.
2. Rueben A. Brower, *The Poetry of Robert Frost: Constellations of Intention* (New York: Oxford University Press, 1963), 26.
3. Cleanth Brooks and Robert Pen Warren, *Understanding Poetry* (Rev. ed.; New York: Henry Holt and Co., 1950), 393.
4. William Bysshe Stein, " 'After Apple-Picking': Echoic Parody," *University Review* (Kansas City, Mo.), XXXV, 301.
5. *Writers at Work*, 28.
6. *Ibid.*, 27.
7. See Brooks and Warren, 394.
8. On this point, see Nina Baym, "An Approach to Robert Frost's Nature Poetry," *Atlantic Quarterly*, XVII (1965), 720. Marion Montgomery, pointing out that Frost is not agnostic, does show that Frost is very much aware of man's limitations and therefore hesitates to speak out "on the subject of the supernatural": "Robert Frost and his Use of Barriers," *South Atlantic Quarterly*, LVII (1958), 343. A. M. Sampley, observing that "Frost does not believe in a directionless universe," nonetheless observes that Frost's men are the sort "who can survive in an uncertain universe": "The Myth and The Quest: The Stature of Robert Frost," *South Atlantic Quarterly*, LXX (1971), 289, 294.
9. Robert Penn Warren, "The Themes of Robert Frost," in *Selected Essays* (New York: Vintage Books, 1951), 130. This essay is a somewhat different form of the analysis appearing in Brooks and Warren.
10. Among others who have discussed the analogy between man and nature, see Phillip L. Gerber, *Robert Frost* (New York: Twayne Publishers, 1966), 133–37.
11. Baym, "An Approach to Robert Frost's Nature Poetry," 716.

*These citations use an older version of MLA format in which endnotes are used for reference.

MARTIN BIDNEY

The Secretive-Playful Epiphanies of Robert Frost: Solitude, Companionship, and the Ambivalent Imagination

Surprisingly, no one has yet tried to find a pattern that can unify the major epiphanies in the poems of Robert Frost; no study of the poet in the last thirty-five years even contains any variant of "epiphany" in its title (though Robert F. Fleissner invokes the related "spot of time"[1]). I seek here to identify the pattern of thematic focuses, recurrent formal feature, and psychological implications unique to Frost's epiphanic style or "signature," his distinctive manner of epiphany-making.[2] Two thematic concerns distinguish the strongest poetic epiphanies of Robert Frost: playfulness[3] and interpersonality. A playful epiphany is an ambivalent one. Because epiphanic moments convey a discovery with deep implications, a playful epiphany creates a conceptual tension, an emotional ambivalence: is the episode a revelation or a mere frivolity? Equally fraught with tension is Frost's awareness that the solitude often required for epiphanic experience must define itself in relation to one's need for social validation. Frost presents his doubly ambivalent epiphanies of playfulness in the conflictual[4] context of the "relational self" (Schapiro).

In *The Ambiguity of Play*, Brian Sutton-Smith distinguishes seven thematic focuses that have helped theorists organize discussions of play: Progress, Fate, Power, Identity, the Imaginary, Self, and Frivolity[5]. These categories have enabled investigators to clarify, respectively, ludic activities as diverse as children's play, games of chance, contests of skill and strategy, festivals and parades, theatrical fantasy, leisure, and humorous nonsense. Every one of Sutton-Smith's seven rubrics illuminates the playful epiphanies of Robert Frost. Progress, Fate, Power, and Frivolity are important but subsidiary. Some of Frost's visions recall stages in the developmental progress whereby a child learns to balance the demands of self and other. Frostian solitaries love to challenge fate and to assert their hard-won visionary power while deprecating their epiphanic achievement with comic whimsy.

But the categories that shed most light on the psychology of Frost's playful epiphanies are the ones Sutton-Smith calls Identity, Self, and the Imaginary. Sutton-Smith sees Identity (what I will call Companionship or Community) as rooted in tradition, community feeling (or *communitas*) and cooperation, forces that validate one's identity or respectability in a social context. Because Sutton-Smith identifies Self with the drive that seeks out individual "peak experiences," I rename it Solitude to emphasize that it empowers Frostian characters' lonely epiphanic searches. And Sutton-Smith's idea of the Imaginary (I call it Imagination) is highly apposite to Frost's playful epiphanic practice.

Frost's playfulness is bound up with the quest for imaginative epiphanies, and Sutton-Smith shows how seriousness and play have been historically linked through Imagination. He connects Imagination to the poetic exuberance of Romanticism and to the satirical dialogism of Bakhtinian carnival, both of which blend seriousness with play: for the philosophic Romanticist Schiller, serious imaginative art was at the same time the most human form of play; obversely, Bakhtin finds the satiric-dialogic mood of carnival gaiety at the root of much serious literary protest. It is not surprising that Frost, well grounded in Romantic tradition, would blend seriousness and play in the epiphanic quest. But to this I would add that, for Frost, the drive toward Solitude and the equally irresistible need for a sense of *communitas*, like seriousness and play, encounter each other in the realm of Imagination. This psychologically crucial encounter, in a Frostian epiphany, is likely to be as *anxiously ambivalent* as it is intense, mysterious, and resonant.

To analyze the ambivalent interpersonal play-epiphanies of Frost I will identify both their subjective and objective features.[6] I define a literary epiphany as an experience felt by the reader to be intense, mysterious, and expansive in meaning—signifying more than such a brief moment would normally have any right to mean.[7] Using this definition of epiphany based on its subjective effects on the reader, I then identify, as objective criteria, recurrent formal features that, taken together, constitute a recognizable pattern unifying a given writer's epiphanic *oeuvre*. These formal indicators, derived from the thinking of phenomenologist Gaston Bachelard, include (1) patterns of motion, (2) elements—in the ancient sense of earth, water, air, and fire, (3) shapes—often linked to elements, as trees are associated with earth or birds with air, (4) colors, including black and white, and (5) sounds and silences. After specifying the component features of Frost's epiphanic pattern, I locate and describe in detail his *paradigm epiphany*, the one privileged moment where the formal features of the pattern are most vividly presented and clearly developed. I devote the remainder of the analysis to more fragmentary or attenuated variants of Frost's paradigm, unfolding their implicit social psychology of epiphanic questing as ambivalent, conflicted play.

The strongest epiphanies of Robert Frost manifest a readily recognizable pattern of motions, shapes, elements, colors, sounds, and silences. The motion pattern features two contrasting types of movement frequently appearing together, as if to symbolize the necessary coexistence and interdependence of the two contrasting attitudes they express: solitary questing and community tradition, imaginative loneliness and companionship.[8] There is, first, the motion of the solitary seeker toward an undefined imaginative goal. In contrast, the person or entity embodying the values of *communitas* or would-be companionship in Frostian epiphanies has three choices: (1) not to move, (2) to move in a direction opposite or contrasting to that of the Solitary, and (3) to pursue the Solitary in a game of *hide-and-seek*, a frequent and favored motion scenario.

No type of Frostian epiphanic movement or immobility can attain its meaning except in contrast with its actual or implicit contrary. The solitary seeker and the collectivity, individual and community, confirm and define each other, though tensions are palpable. Frostian players of hide-and-seek are never "caught" except on their own terms or by their own consent. Yet solitude and companionship, the reclusive independence of the poetic wanderer (option A) and the conventional security of *communitas* (option B), need not be embodied in distinct persons in a Frostian epiphany. Instead, the two tendencies or "voices" often compete within the mind of a single epiphanist-persona who hovers playfully and guiltily between them—like "voices" of rebellious independence and parental caution in the mind of a growing child.

Frostian epiphanic shapes can be quasi-geometrical, natural forms, or barely definable flashings, flutters, or gleams. The predominant geometric shape in a Frostian epiphany is a rounded, circular, or cylindrical enclosure, formed by a tunnel, a well, a dark pool, a fern wreath, or trees in a forest. At times the dark closure may take a squarish outline, such as a dark house, or even a grey woodpile felt to contain a hidden, slow-burning fire. Among natural and nature-like forms, Frost favors trees and birds, or a birdlike white wave or fluttering book page. A single tree may be the locus or agent of a revelation, or a group of trees may be the epiphanic site.[9] Birds, associated with trees, are central to Frostian epiphany; Frost makes the two images evoke each other, and he links birds and trees to music. Lastly, Frost favors sudden flashings, flutters, or gleams of whiteness, often in dark enclosures or on dark backgrounds, and often related to his birds and waves.

Fascinated by the indefinable or ambivalent, Frost may blend sound with silence in his epiphanies. As just noted, birds and trees suggest music: panpipes appear as a forest emblem or "sylvan sign," and even morning-glory vines, a diminutive thicket, recall harp strings. Yet, paradoxically, silence—or the muffling of sound—may be as crucial of these epiphanies as music. The poet's song may be "swallowed up" by a throatlike enclosure of trees, or a distant violin may be heard, or a woman may have "on her lips" a song "only to herself," or pipes may be muted as a new music is pondered. We hear enigmatic or conflicted combinations or blendings of song and silence. Frost may use white noise—the rushing of leaves—to bridge sound and silence, music and tonelessness. Indefinability, indeterminacy, and the linking of opposite ideas open an area where limits are questioned, an ambivalent liminal zone or epiphanic border-realm.

The elements of earth, air, water, and fire interrelate in Frostian epiphanies. Earth predominates because of the sylvan emphasis; woods are abundant. Air is associated with birds, with the rustling music of tree branches, with the breath of song, or with the breath of spirit, of silence. An eddy in a pool may take on a strangely aery, birdlike epiphanic shape. And an abandoned woodpile may seem to burn, warming the forest with its hidden Heraclitean fire of decay. So all four elements contribute to the revelation of the Frostian reclusive seeker.

Just as Frost juxtaposes sound and silence in the ambivalent enclosure of his epiphanies, so, too, he shows a kind of elemental ambiguity embodied in glass, seemingly a solid but really a liquid in suspension. Combining brightness and colorlessness, transparency and reflected light, glass embodies a questioning of categorical limits, a material ambivalence. Frost varies the epiphanic theme of glass as water-mirror, crystal, and quartz, or—audibly—in the crystalline timbre of bells.

Frost, who loves indefinability, can question the limits of tonal and elemental categories, respectively, through the use of a sonar border-concept suggesting indeterminacy (the white noise or pitchless tones of rustling leaves) and by the ambivalent combination of vivid brightness and empty transparency in the solid-liquid anomaly of glass. He similarly questions color categories by making his epiphanic moments chiefly a matter of black, the non-color, and/or white, the all-color. (Sometimes the more indeterminate idea of invisibility may substitute for the negative notion of darkness or blackness.) An indeterminate, fluttering or vacillating, birdlike or wavelike white object may appear in a black enclosure, a tunnel, a well, a dark pool. Or a black enclosure may be starkly contrasted with a surrounding or adjacent whiteness (woods on a snowy evening). The category-questioning, the indeterminate, the all-or-nothing, the all-and-nothing—such is the focus of a Frostian ambivalent epiphany of blackness or invisibility, and/or blank, riddling whiteness.

I have stressed that Frostian solitary epiphanic seeking and community tradition, loneliness and sociability, define each other and thus imply each other by vivid contrast. But we also find in Frost a kind of attempted epiphanic compromise, a shared epiphany that is Solitary- or recluse-friendly, experienced by a select group—sometimes of three persons, like a nuclear family. In such revelatory if transient, always ambivalent compromise between the demands of solitude and society, a black-white contrast may no longer be required: a suspensefully irresolute, erect white "leaf" of an open book may be observed in a lighted room. Shared recluse-friendly epiphanies may show large areas of light: a silver cloud approaches a refulgent moon.

The ambivalent playfulness of the poetic seeker in a Frostian epiphany may involve willfulness, whimsy, mockery, caprice, or teasing—often a teasing secretiveness. Though we find in Frost a few privileged moments of relaxed and playful love, the playfulness in his epiphanies is more commonly of a troubled and troubling kind: it may be prankish, mischievous,[10] defiant, ironic, sarcastic, irresponsible, dangerous, even seemingly cruel. It may include feelings of guilt or profanation, at times engendering a twinge—or surge—of regret, an impulse to repent. Frost embodies the playful-epiphanic intermixture of disturbing ironies with appealing imaginative daring in variants of the myth of the willful or mischievous poet-child-god: satire-satyr Pan, self-enwreathed Narcissus.

"A Dream Pang," Frost's playful, interpersonal epiphanic paradigm, displays—in a characteristic mood of intense ambivalence and uneasy equivocation—his recurrent motion pattern (hide-and-seek), shape (enclosure of trees), and interactive elements (woods and wind), his ambivalent blendings of sound and silence (muffled song, white noise of leaves), and the equally central related theme of invisibility. The oneiric power of this oddly unregarded[11] dialogic dream sonnet is exemplary, as is the Frostian dialogue between the perspectives of the would-be Companion in the opening octet and the would-be Solitary in the sestet's antiphonal response. The two-part epiphany is a play scenario involving secretiveness and pursuit, hide-and-seek:

I had withdrawn in forest, and my song
Was swallowed up in leaves that blew away;

And to the forest edge you came one day
(This was my dream) and looked and pondered long
But did not enter, though the wish was strong.
You shook your pensive head as who should say,
"I dare not—too far in his footsteps stray—
He must seek me would he undo the wrong." (1-8)

The dream game is by no means pure pleasure. It may be narcissisti-
cally gratifying that the Companion purportedly has such a strong wish
to enter the forest where the Solitary is hiding. But this powerful desire
of the Companion may be merely fantasized, while the enunciated
reproach is all too real. The Companion's reluctance to "dare" to enter the
forest may seem timid, but the reproof is bold: the Solitary has strayed
from the true path and must "undo" such a "wrong." This accusation may
be a spouse's or a lover's, but it sounds more like a parent's reprimand
stipulating how a child must rectify the offense he has committed; one
readily imagines the early childhood origin of the tense dream scenario.[12] Not only is the Solitary made to feel guilty in relation to an
authoritative Companion, but even the poetic achievement he has
effected through his solitude is highly equivocal: the swallowing of his
song in the leaves, as if in the dark cylindrical throat of the forest,
threateningly renders the poet mute. But perpetually blowing leaves
can magically make a lovely, quasi-musical rushing sound, and the Solitary may well feel comfortable surrounded by this waterlike white noise,
auditory insulation from unwelcome human company. In the sestet we
hear his revealing equivocal reply to the proffered charge of aloofness:

Not far, but near, I stood and saw it all:
Behind low boughs the trees let down outside;
And the sweet pang it cost me not to call
And tell you that I saw does still abide.
But 'tis not true that thus I dwelt aloof,
For the wood wakes, and you are here for proof. (9-14)

The singer admits a continuing sense of guilt, or at least regret. Yet he
rejects the imputation of willful coldness. The waking of the wood may
mean that the slumbrous dream was not real anyway; that daytime reality has now supervened, replacing defiance with pleasant companionship. Yet the waking of the dream-wood may equally well mean that the
nocturnal rebellion was real and that its reality survives into daytime—

that the poet's triumphant, secretive defiance in the dream was real then and is real now. The guiltily playful epiphanist-persona, like a rebellious growing child, is torn between apology and apologia.

Everything about this playful-disturbing paradigmatic dream epiphany is uneasily ambivalent. The enclosure of trees muting the poet's voice is potentially incapacitating but reassuringly protective, too, of the Solitary's fragile independence. The kind of movement in Option A is bolder, more exploratory, than that of Option B; the Solitary dares to venture into the dark enclosure, while the Companion does not. The Solitary will not allow himself to be caught except by his own consent, and only in the fantasy context of a concluded dream. His song may be silenced for a while, but the white noise of rustling boughs may well betoken an initiatory entry into a privileged oneiric if ambiguous realm of subtler, more puzzling poetic music.[13] Yet when the dream forest awakens, the rebellious quester, too, will, awake to a sobering realization: no Solitary can be a poet without help of a hearer. In his conflicted epiphany scenario, the maturing singer demands respect yet feels partly culpable, not wholly secure. Using the categories of Sutton-Smith, we may say that in this playfulness the Solitary has shown Progress toward independence, has asserted Power, has dared Fate, and has courted the charge of Frivolity. Most important, Imagination has produced an epiphany of mysterious, intense if unstable power by playing Solitude against Companionship or *communitas*. The dream ritual has tested the Solitary's power to tease out or provoke the acceptance, or love, of his importunate, baffled Companion.

NOTES

1. " 'Spot of Time' in Frost: Beddoes, Vaughan—or Wordsworth in 'Stopping by Woods'?" *Robert Frost Review* (Fall 1993): 24–28.

2. Seven of Frost's ten best epiphanic poems are found in *A Boy's Will* (1913), *North of Boston* (1914), and *Mountain Interval* (1916). The other three are "Stopping by Woods on a Snowy Evening" and "For Once, Then, Something," both from *New Hampshire* (1923), and the title poem of *West-Running Brook* (1928). Beginning roughly with the 1928 book and with *A Further Range* (1936), Frost's "very manner of voice changes. Metaphorical indirection gives way to explicit generalization. The forms of satirical discourse and epigram are introduced to convey his opinion more directly. The poet's old game of hide-and-seek is still evident but now is carried on more by means of a bantering verbal irony" (Ogilvie 73–4). I build here on Ogilvie's seminal remark regarding the "hide-and-seek" tactic.

3. Citing the couplet "It takes all sorts in- and outdoor-schooling / To get adapted to my kind of fooling," Cook sees Frost "playing perilously at the confluence of

opposing forces" (222, 235). Edwards (245) finds Frost most playful in animal anthropomorphism; for Beacham (246) his play centers on irony.

4. Faggen (2) contrasts such critics as Trilling and Jarrell, who saw "terror" in Frost, with more recent writers (Poirier, Oster, Monteiro) for whom Frost is "less a terrifying poet than a playfully ironic one." Focusing on conflict in Frost's epiphanies, I intend *not* to slight terror in favor of play.

5. See especially 214–31 for summary paraphrased here.

6. See my other work on epiphanies: "The Aestheticist Epiphanies of J. D. Salinger: Bright-Hued Circles, Spheres, and Patches; 'Elemental' Joy and Pain." *Style* 34 (2000): 117–31; " 'Controlled Panic': Mastering the Terrors of Dissolution and Isolation in Elizabeth Bishop's Epiphanies." *Style* 34 (2000): 487–511; "Failed Verticals, Fatal Horizontals, Unreachable Circles of Light: Phillip Larkin's Epiphanies." *Moments of Moment: Aspects of the Literary Epiphany.* Ed Wim Tigges. Amsterdam: Rodopi P, 1999. 353–74; *Patterns of Epiphany: From Wordsworth to Tolstoy, Pater, and Barrett Browning.* Carbondale: Southern Illinois UP, 1997.

7. My second and third criteria are borrowed from Ashton Nichols's *The Poetics of Epiphany: Nineteenth-Century Origins of the Modern Literary Moment* (Tuscaloosa: U of Alabama P, 1987) 28.

8. My emphasis here parallels that of Richardson (3–4) on Frost's "decision not to weight the values" of "rebellion and conformity" or Dionysus and Apollo as "one-sidedly" in favor of Dionysian rebellion as Mencken had done, but rather to locate tendencies toward both change and permanence in every individual.

9. Ogilvie (65) has noted the poet's "preoccupation" with "the recurrent image, particularly in his earlier work, of dark woods and trees." "The necessity for participating in both worlds, the worlds of self-in-society and self-in-seclusion, sets up a rhythm of continual advance and retreat which informs Frost's entire poetic expression. 'Trees' and 'mankind' are alternately sought and avoided as circumstances direct" (67)—an insight I build on here. Ogilvie shows how trees yield to the imagery of stars as the poetry later becomes more generalized and impersonal (74).

10. Muldoon (128) cites Frost's letter to Leonidas W Payne Jr., 1 November 1927, acknowledging "my innate mischievousness."

11. Maxson, who repeatedly misreads "blew alway" as "blew away," finds this poem "not of uppermost importance among the sonnets" of Frost (31). Other critics barely mention it.

12. For Maxson (31) this poem "introduces the male/female, husband/wife conflicts and relationships that would be featured so prominently in *North of Boston* and beyond." But when, after the dream, the speaker says that "the wood wakes, and you are here for proof" (14), the word "here" doesn't have to mean "here in the bed," though Oster (145), too, speaks confidently about "the physical presence of his wife in their bed." The first few times I read "A Dream Pang" I envisioned the poet's mother standing in the doorway. If the poem does depict a husband-wife relationship, it is one that seems closely patterned on the way a child may feel in relation to a parent: vulnerable, rebellious, defensive, yet ready to fantasize a peace pact.

13. Squires (49), in a comment on the speaker's withdrawal into the swallowing leaves, notes that although the poem's first two lines "suggest that in being lost in nature Frost feels a loss of self, or at least some challenge to the self," the "moment when bearings disappear is often also a fructifying moment."

WORKS CITED

Beacham, Walton. "Technique and the Sense of Play in the Poetry of Robert Frost," Frost: Centennial Essays II. Ed. Jac Tharpe. Jackson: UP of Mississippi, 1976. 246–61.

Faggen, Robert, Robert Frost and the Challenge of Darwin. Ann Arbor: U of Michigan P, 1997.

Frost, Robert. Collect Poems, Prose, and Plays. Ed. with annotations by Richard Poirier and Mark Richardson. New York: Lib. of Amer., 1995.

Maxson, H. A. On the Sonnets of Robert Frost. Jefferson, NC: McFarland, 1997.

Muldoon, Paul. "Notes Towards an Ars Poetica." Essays in Criticism 48 (1998): 107–28.

Ogilvie, John T. "From Woods to Stars: A Pattern of Imagery in Robert Frost's Poetry." South Atlantic Quarterly 58 (1959): 64–76.

Oster, Judith. Toward Robert Frost: The Reader and the Poet. Athens: U of Georgia P, 1991.

Richardson, Mark. The Ordeal of Robert Frost: The Poet and His Poetics. Urbana: U of Illinois P, 1997.

Schapiro, Barbara Ann. Literature and the Relational Self. New York: New York UP, 1994.

Squires, Radcliffe. The Major Themes of Robert Frost. Ann Arbor: U of Michigan P, 1969.

Sutton-Smith, Brian. The Ambiguity of Play. Cambridge: Harvard UP, 1997.

DONALD J. GREINER

"That Plain-Speaking Guy": A Conversation with James Dickey on Robert Frost

The following conversation took place December 15, 1972, in Columbia, South Carolina. Very much aware of the occasion of Robert Frost's upcoming centennial, James Dickey was eager to talk about the artist whose work, he said, has meant very much to him. The conversation was punctuated with reading and witty asides, the most important of which are included below. Neither Mr. Dickey nor I was concerned with interpretations of individual poems. The entire conversation focused upon the more general questions about what makes Robert Frost a great poet and why his poems continue to invite serious reading.

GREINER: We're talking about a poet who was born a hundred years ago; I'm wondering how you would evaluate his status now that he's been dead for more than a decade. In other words, today, are these poems dated; is his poetry the kind that younger poets are going to repudiate the way he rejected the rhythms of a Tennyson or Swinburne?

DICKEY: No, I don't think so. Frost is a poet that the younger fellows may reject and turn their back on, and so on, but he is a poet whom people are going to come back to. Which is to say that he is real poet; he's arrived to stay.

GREINER: Your comment suggests that his poems appeal to readers and not particularly to beginning writers. Do his poems have anything to show beginning writers today? I mean, you're teaching students who hope to be poets . . . .

DICKEY: Oh, a very great deal to show them. The plainness and the colloquialism of the language is a very great plus. And for a certain kind of poet, a poet who's learning to write, this may be the way for him.

GREINER: Do you think his poems still speak to the American reader today the way they did maybe twenty or even fifty years ago? Frost was worshipped.

DICKEY: Well, you'll have to dissociate . . . you have to distinguish in the first place between the actual poem and the public personality of the man. And it's hard to make any kind of reasonable assessment of that because the majority of people who revered Robert Frost had read very little of his work.

GREINER: Right, they read only the anthology pieces.

DICKEY: Well, and not even that. No, they only knew him as a public figure, you know, a consultant at the Library of Congress, someone who gave forth with "frosty," if I may be forgiven a pun, saws and cracker-barrel wisdom and things of that nature. But they, mostly the people who I would say—and God knows I don't know what the percentage would be—but ninety, I would say ninety percent of the people who knew who Robert Frost was would never have read any poems of his.

GREINER: Do you think we ought to reread his poems, or should his poems . . . put it this way . . . should his poems be reevaluated now in the light of what we know about Frost the man?

DICKEY: Oh, I don't think so. I'm fascinated by Frost the man, and he certainly must have been one of the worst sons-of-bitches that ever lived. But what really matters is what ends up on the page—what he did as an artist.

GREINER: In your essay in *Babel to Byzantium* you've mentioned the "Frost story."

DICKEY: (laughter) Yeah.

GREINER: I'm wondering, will it ever be possible for us to read "The Gift Outright," say, without thinking of the context of President Kennedy's inauguration; or could we ever read "Birches" or "Mending Wall" or any other of what you call his "beloved" poems without remembering Frost on the grandstand before the worshipful audience, cracking up those in the front row with his little asides? Is it possible that there . . . ?

DICKEY: That's an awful hard question to answer. This is getting exactly back to my point. There's a dissociation between the man and his public image and what he actually did put down on the page. He's a remarkable poet. But he became a personality. And I don't think—I mean, I agree with you—I don't think there really will, at least in our generation, be the possibility of dividing Frost the raconteur and the public personality from the man who wrote some *very marvelous* poems.

GREINER: You know, I think in a perverse way that the negative information, which we now know about Frost may eventually help his reputation as a poet. I know students who have been turned off by this image of the white-haired old bard of the nation, who now say, well, this guy really was. . . .

DICKEY: He was human after all.

GREINER: Right. He was not "preachy." He had problems.

DICKEY: And he created most of them himself. [laughter] But he's . . . those Lawrance Thompson biographies—those books are fascinating because you get the dichotomy between the poems as they have come to exist in innumerable anthologies and so on and what went into the poems. I'm very high on literary biographies myself. I was fascinated by those books.

GREINER: They're excellent books. I hope he lives to finish the third volume.

DICKEY: Well, I think it will be finished from what I've learned— the information that I have. But maybe not by him.

GREINER: One more question in this line of though. Do you think, maybe, in his, in Frost's last years—now this is speculation obviously—do you think he was pursuing finally the reputation more than the art?

DICKEY: Yes, I do. I definitely do.

GREINER: To turn to another idea. In you essay on Frost in *Babel to Byzantium*, you mention "Design," "After Apple-Picking," "Provide, Provide," and "To Earthward" as "a few powerful and utterly original poems." A marvelous way to describe them. Would you revise that list today?

DICKEY: I might put a few more, but I wouldn't take out any of those.

GREINER: Okay, that's fair enough. In the same essay you mention Frost's, what you call his technical triumph, a triumph of the highest kind. You define it as "the creation of a particular kind of poetry-speaking voice." Yet I note in your list of those four poems that you neither discuss nor name one of the longer dialogue poems in which he literally does have a person speaking. Do these poems seem—a poem like "Home Burial"—do these poems seem startling still, today?

DICKEY: "Home Burial" is a mighty good poem. But when I talk about a special kind of poetry-speaking voice, I don't mean that someone . . . that someone speaking the poem (whatever the word is), a persona is—necessarily has to be—involved. That's not what I mean. If I didn't get that point across. . . .

GREINER: No, you got it across. My point is that these poems—"Home Burial," "Hired Man"—my point is that when Frost hit it big in England and the United States in 1913, 1914, 1915, he was making it with the so-called dialogue poems which were misread as free verse. I'm wondering if today these poems are no longer—obviously they're not as revolutionary—if they're no longer as interesting, or if they no longer seem as technically innovative? I'm thinking of a poem like "Death of the Hired Man," or "The Fear," or "Home Burial."

DICKEY: Well, I don't know. I really wouldn't be able to pronounce on that because I'm pretty close to the poems, and they've meant a lot to me over the years. What they mean to this generation or that generation or for this reason or that is really not of any particular concern to me. To me personally.

GREINER: You say that Frost—and I agree—you say that Frost is at his best when he's "most rhythmical and cryptic." Are you referring to his well-known love of hinting, of metaphor? He was obsessed with metaphor.

DICKEY: Yes. Yes, he was. But the thing about Frost that makes him so good is that he's able to say the most amazing things without seeming to raise his voice.

GREINER: That's very well put. A poem like "The Most of It" would then. . . . I remember that Yvor Winters didn't like Frost's poetry but thought highly of "The Most of It."

DICKEY: Well, he didn't think *very* highly of it. But he didn't think very highly of Frost. Yet he liked that poem except that he then proceeded to pick it apart in the most pretentious terms. Let me read this because I don't think that this is a very well-known quote, and it's very quotable. Tom Priestly, J. B. Priestly's son, was the cutter on my movie, the film editor. An he sent me this [*Literature and Western Man*]. I've read it—I've just about read it to pieces, but it's a very good assessment, I think, of Frost. Let's see. Priestly says Frost "is widely recognised as a major poet and is altogether an odd, original, unexpected figure. His poetry is, in his own phrase, 'versed in country matters'; it is not even national but local, New England in scene and manner; it is as frugal with imagery and metaphor as a farmer with his money [laughter]; much of it appears to have a rhythm and tone of cautious conversation, spoken out of the side of the mouth by a man not looking at you—" [laughter]

GREINER: That's good.

DICKEY: "Yet through this stealthy rusticity comes almost everything, short of the depths of personal dissolution and the blazing heights of ecstasy, that the modern poet is trying to express—bewilderment and horror, wonder and compassion, a tragic sense of life, which he, however, suggests without bitterness or whining. This is a poet, using his poker-faced rural *persona*, who likes to pretend he is being simple and obvious when he is not, just as many other poets, going with the movement, like to pretend they are being profound when they are not."

GREINER: That's nicely expressed. The idea about the modern strikes me. To continue from what Priestly says, Frost, as you know, for years was criticized as a leftover nineteenth-century poet, as a watered-down Emerson. . . .

DICKEY: Or Wordsworth [laughter].

GREINER: Right. As a man who should be back in the 1850's. Do you think it's Frost's dark vision that makes him modern, one of the qualities that makes him modern since his verse form may not be?

DICKEY: I don't know about that. But I do think that the speech which Lionel Trilling made about him, which I quoted in my article—Frost as a poet of darkness and terror, fear—the motivating emotion in him was fear—is the correct Frost.

GREINER: I would agree. You know, that speech wasn't made until 1959; and while I'm sure isolated readers here and there recognized the element of fear, as you call it, or terror in Frost, for years he was considered a benign nature poet, a goody goody, the kind of poet read to the Camellia Garden Club.

DICKEY: Yeah, those readers might have his face put up on Mount Rushmore [laughter].

GREINER: Exactly, with his hair fluffed up [laughter]. I'm wondering, have we only recently discovered these dark poems? Is it because the critic is always lagging behind the poet, or is it because in our age of continuing crisis these poems are now speaking to us more and more—"Neither Out Far nor In Deep," for example?

DICKEY: Yes, I think that's very well said. The best critic, the critic who has understood Frost most deeply was Randall Jarrell.

GREINER: Yes, his work is wonderfully perceptive.

DICKEY: Because Jarrell was something of the same type of man. And he understood the depths under the still pools, you know.

GREINER: He's the one who wrote the long discussion of "Home Burial." What about Frost's wit? his humor? Do you think poems like—I'm just throwing out some—like—"October" or "One Step Backward Taken" or "Fire and Ice"—I'm not thinking of his less-successful attempts to be funny in those awful "editorials"—do you think those poems have a place in the final assessment of Frost?

DICKEY: Well, that is the Frost who has kind of an elephantine local New England humor. The ponderous attempt to be funny and witty is the Frost that I can most easily dispense with, you know.

GREINER: Most readers dismiss the "cute" Frost of the "editorials."

DICKEY: The Frost I like is the plain-speaking guy who can in the most conversational possible way say things that you wouldn't have thought of in a million years.

GREINER: You know, talking about the common way of saying something, I find so many students today relishing, understandably, Stevens, or Eliot . . . I'm thinking of the more famous modern poets . . . or Pound, and dismissing Frost, until they come upon a poem like "All Revelation" or "Directive." And I'm wondering if the so-called easier poems like "Stopping by Woods" or "Birches" have been so over-anthologized, so over-taught that students no longer respond to them and therefore end up with a warped view of Frost's achievement.

DICKEY : As a university professor, as you are, Don, I have become—I couldn't speak for you, but I can certainly speak for myself—I have become very wary and mistrustful of this insistent, universal "talking it" to death. Talking things to death. We are paid to do it, but as far as the art of poetry is concerned I have very serious reservations as to whether or not this is desirable.

GREINER: This is what's happened, I think, to a poem like "Birches" or "Mending Wall" or "Stopping by Woods."

DICKEY: Well, that's what you have when you say you "get" a poet like Frost who's well known, who's taught, as they say, "in classes."

GREINER: And who has an easy literal level.

DICKEY: You get lots of people who get to competing in interpreting him.

GREINER: You remember that Frost's famous comment about "Stopping by Woods" was "All I meant was to get the hell out of there."

DICKEY: Yeah? Well, he was right. Certainly. You read the commentaries on those things and they're so over-read and over-ingenious and so on that the poem just gets mangled and destroyed in the process.

GREINER: Someone in the late '50's or early '60's, I understand, actually counted and decided that "Stopping by Woods" is the most explicated poem in American literature, that it's been "done" so many more times. . . .

DICKEY: Well, but of course it's got to contain a homosexual Freudian overtone, undertone, all that kind of business, you know, . . . uh! [laughter] It's just a hideous business. But the poetry, the fun of it, the delight of it, dies when you indulge this over-intellectualizing about it.

GREINER: I like the way Frost hits me with a unexpected word. For example, to pull one out of the hat, in "Fire and Ice," when ice "is also great/And would suffice"—the word "suffice," for example, surprises me, that kind of thing.

DICKEY: Yes, I agree, that's good.

GREINER: Some critics have argued persuasively that Frost is a good poet but not one to be read finally with Yeats or Stevens or Eliot. Now, get the reason: because he did not develop what they call a coherent vision or myth, and because he oversimplifies human experience by writing about modern crises from the vantage point of the rural world. Are those criticism justified in your opinion?

DICKEY: Not in my opinion, no. I think that he has one virtue that overrides all of those things, and that is that he speaks to people on a very deep level. He speaks to them in a language they can understand, but the meanings of the lines in his poems go very deeply down. He's not a recherché kind of writer like Stevens who is always dealing in riddles and conundrums and that sort of thing. Frost has a great, great, wide spread on the popular world. He shows us here in America that a poet does not have to talk down to his audience, but that he can talk to his audience with condescending.

GREINER: The literal level in my opinion does not hurt Frost at all.

DICKEY: No, I think that's one of the best thing's he's got going for him.

GREINER: I have so many sophisticated graduate students, though, who feel that he is less than great because of the literal level.

DICKEY: That's one of the finest things about him. I mean you take Wallace Stevens and you keep going round and round in circles, trying to follow his thought and so on, and it's poetry of a very sophisticate esthete. Frost, whether or not you accept him, is a plain-speaking man, and you are interested in what he says because you can relate to it, whereas you cannot relate to "sixteen ways of putting a pineapple together" [laughter].

GREINER: This would also account, of course, for Frost's very, very broad audience.

DICKEY: Right! He furnishes the figure of the poet in American life who can speak plainly and deeply at the same time.

GREINER: In your reading of Frost—I'm thinking of all of Frost—do you detect any development, change . . . trying out new things, or would you agree with those who argue that he develops, shows his all in *North of Boston*, which was published in 1914, and from there on out his poems go in generally a straight line?

DICKEY: Yes, I do agree with the latter.

GREINER: That's his serious drawback?

DICKEY: In a way, yes. He never learned the great lesson of Picasso, which was never to be trapped in a single style. He found a single style, and he used it and explored it for the rest of his life. But he was not a man who operated on the frontiers of consciousness, who was trying new things and doing new, such as Picasso, who was continually trying to push out the boundaries of human consciousness. He found one thing that he could do. He didn't try to go out; he tried to go in, to go deeper into what he had already found. And that's another type of writer from somebody like Ezra Pound or Auden who do try to do these new things.

GREINER: How would you define that one thing? Is that a fair question? He found "one thing."

DICKEY: Well, it's a—to come back to what I said earlier—a plain-speaking style which could say profound things.

GREINER: He tried in later years, you know, to move into satire, political commentaries. . . .

DICKEY: Didn't work! No, and there he engaged the worst side of himself which was this elephantine levity and this cracker-barrel philosophizing which is not only unpleasant but painful.

GREINER: One poem of Frost's—I would hesitate to say he was "done" in his early life—but "Directive" which was published in, what, 1947? saves his later poetry for me.

DICKEY: Yes, that's a good poem, and "Provide, Provide" is a wonderful poem. It's a wonderful poem! Boy, I'll tell you . . . when you read Frost, when you read that poem and you read some of the others of about that time, you know the full horror of being a human being, you know, and the real practicality and the practical solutions of how you provide for yourself.

GREINER: A better "proletarian" poem than those by some of the proletarian writers.

DICKEY: Oh, yes, far, far better.

GREINER: Let me ask you one final question which is strictly personal opinion. If—one of these "if" questions—if you had room to include one or two of Frost's poems in a world anthology, right off the top of your head, which ones would you pick?

DICKEY: Of Frost?

GREINER: Yes.

DICKEY: Oh, I'd say "Acquainted with the Night" and "After Apple-Picking."

WILLIAM MEREDITH

In Memory of Robert Frost

(1988)

Everyone had to know something, and what they said
About that, the thing they'd learned by curious heart,
They said well.
            That was what he wanted to hear,
Something you had done too exactly for words,
Maybe, but too exactly to lie about either.
Compared to such talk, most conversation
Is inadvertent, low-keyed lying.

If he walked in fear of anything, later on
(Except death, which he died with a healthy fear of)
It was that he would misspeak himself. Even his smile
He administered with some care, accurately.
You could not put words in his mouth
And when you quoted him in his presence
There was no chance that he would not contradict you.

Then there were apparent samenesses he would not
Be deceived by. The presidents of things,
Or teachers, braggarts, poets

Might offer themselves in stereotype
But he would insist on paying attention
Until you at least told him an interesting lie.
(That was perhaps your field of special knowledge?)
The only reason to lie, he said, was for a purpose:
To get something you wanted that bad.

I told him a couple—to amuse him,
To get something I wanted, his attention?
More likely, respite from the blinding attention,
More likely, a friendship
I felt I could only get by stealing.

What little I'd learned about flying
Must have sweated my language lean. *I'd respect you
For that if for nothing else*, he said not smiling
The time I told him, thirty-two night landings
On a carrier, or thirty-two night catapult shots—
Whatever it was, true, something I knew.

Sample Student
Research Paper

Tanguay 1

Pablo Tanguay

Introduction to Literature

Dr. Petersen

4 July 2003

Imagination as Transcendence in Robert Frost

In much of Robert Frost's poetry, the overriding theme **Introduction of topic**
is that we live in the natural world but are basically uncon-
nected to it. He is not, however, overly pessimistic about this;
while the gap between nature and man causes Thomas Hardy to feel
despair, for Frost this separation provides him with the chance
to talk about the poet's greatest gift: the imagination. For
Frost, imagination itself takes on the role of spirit, force,
religion. In "Birches" and in "Two Look at Two," Frost charac-
terizes the imagination as a *transporter*. While it cannot drop **Thesis statement**
us off into the center of some natural Eden and leave us there
forever, these poems show that it can, for a while anyway, take
us *toward* Eden, *toward* nature. Speaking to <u>New York Times</u>
<u>Magazine</u> in 1959, Frost said, "Just as I feel I never have to go
to sleep, little dreams begin to come over me—voices sometimes—
and I know I am gone. There is a curious connection between
reverie, meditation, and dreams" (Bracker 43).

In "Birches," Frost seems to offer a metaphor for seeking
that dreamlike experience of nature. Frank Lentricchia, in **Expert opinion as evidence**
"The Redemptive Imagination," writes that "The movement [in
'Birches'] into transcendence is a movement into a realm of
radical imaginative freedom . . ." (107). The poem propels a
young boy, "too far from town to learn baseball, / Whose only
play was what he found himself" (26-27), up a birch tree, **Primary source as evidence**
climbing "To the top branches" (36). From there, above the
tops of trees, well above the concerns of the earth, Frost has

Tanguay 2

the boy immediately "flung outward, feet first, with a swish, /
Kicking his way down through the air to the ground" (39-40).

The boy climbing his father's birch tree and swinging
down on its pliable branches is the central image of the
poem, but a look back at the text reveals a somewhat surprising fact: the action itself—from ground to "above the
brim" (38) and back to ground—occurs in just five and a half
lines of the fifty-nine-line poem. An even closer look, however, reveals a bigger surprise: there is no boy at all, no
climbing of the tree, no "learn[ing] all there was / To learn
about" (32-33). Within the poem itself, the poem's speaker
imagines the entire scenario. "I like to think some boy's been
swinging them" (3), he says early on, and adds later, just
before the climbing episode, "I should prefer to have some boy
bend them" (23). The central metaphor of the poem, therefore,
is something imagined, and thus it reinforces Frost's point
that the imagination enables a person to experience a
transcendent reality.

Analysis of central image in poem

Frost is careful, though, not to let the boy climbing the
tree remain too out of touch with the human world for too long.
As noted above, even in the speaker's imagination, the boy is
immediately plunged back down to solid ground. Eric Carl Link
notes that Frost certainly "express[es] a certain skepticism
concerning the ability of the poet to reconcile man and
Nature . . ." (183). But this temporary flight of the speaker's
imagination is what allows the speaker to bear the reality of
"Truth [breaking] in / With all her matter-of-fact" (21-22).
The speaker says, "But swinging doesn't bend them down to stay.
/ Ice storms do that" (4-5). In the final third of the poem, he
openly admits his imaginative conceit: "So I was once a swinger
of birches," he says, "And so dream of going back to be"
(41-42). It is at the point of alienation, "when we are weary

Tanguay 3

of considerations / And life is too much like a pathless wood"
(43-44), Frost is saying, that we seek transcendence, and the
transcendence comes in the seeking, which is in the domain of
the imagination. The speaker wants to "go by climbing a birch
tree" (54) "*Toward* heaven" (56), but to be returned because
"Earth's the right place for love" (52). And, in a world of ice
storms, what is more human and imaginative than love?

In "Two Look at Two," as in "Birches," the speaker's
imagination transforms simple observation into an experience
of transcendence. The speaker here, though, unlike the first-
person narrator in "Birches," is an outside observer, someone
uninvolved in the action. The poem's characters—a man and
woman, a buck and doe—provide the action, but it is the speaker
who interprets that action, and it is thus the speaker's
imagination that is the overriding force in the poem. "Two Look
at Two" is about human willingness to allow the imagination to
transform an ordinary human-nature encounter into a magical
event.

Analysis of narrative perspective in poem

The poem's "plot" is simple enough: a man and a woman,
hiking on a trail at dusk, encounter across "a tumbled wall /
With barbed-wire binding" (7-8) first a doe, then a buck.
From the moment of encounter, though, the point of view shifts
from the human couple to the deer couple, and we see the event
(as interpreted by the speaker) from the perspective of the
deer. This transformation of perspective allows Frost to play
with perception—that is, to show us man from the point of view
of nature. And from nature's perspective, man is not very
interesting, or lively, or even dangerous. The speaker
interprets the doe's thoughts: "Then, as if they were something
that, though strange / She could not trouble her mind with too
long, / She sighed and passed unscared along the wall" (22-24).
The buck is actually disdainful, saying to the couple, "Why

Tanguay 4

don't you make some motion? / Or give some sign of life?
Because you can't. / I doubt if you're as living as you look"
(32-34). To the human couple, however, the encounter is
profoundly important, and after the poem shifts back to the
human point of view, we learn that the encounter "Had made them
certain earth returned their love" (42).

What is interesting here beyond the shift in perspective, however, is the same twist Frost employs in
"Birches": while the landscape is real, the crux of the
narrative is fictional. Deer do not think like humans, nor do
they speak. Martin Bidney's essay "The Secretive-Playful
Epiphanies of Robert Frost" makes note of, among other things,
the "uneasily ambivalent" nature of Frost's work (60), and
this scene's blending of the imaginative and the real is no
exception. In fact, Frost lets us know fairly blatantly that
the deer's thoughts and feelings are imagined. He does this by
using qualifiers when he presents the deer's words and
imaginings: "She [the doe] *seemed* to think" (21); "*as if* they
were something" (22); "*As if* to ask" (32).

At the same time, though, Frost does not subject the
deer's physical movements to qualification, fully investing
them with human characteristics: "She [the doe] *sighed* and
passed *unscared*" (24); "He [the buck] viewed them *quizzically*"
(31); "Then he too passed *unscared*" (37). The language
describing the human couple also wavers between qualification
("Love and forgetting *might* have carried them" [1]; "*As if* the
earth . . . / had made them certain" [42-44]) and objective
description ("With thoughts of the path back, how rough it was"
[5]). This description is the speaker's way of connecting the
couples, his imaginative attempt to tie together man and
nature, but Frost the poet is all too aware that the connection
is at best temporary, which is why he builds in the discrepancy

*Discussion of
imagination in
the poem*

*Discussion of
personification in
the poem*

Tanguay 5

of perception between the deer couple and human couple. As with
the boy needing to return to solid ground in "Birches," so too
must the human couple in "Two Look at Two" turn back and go
home. To Frost, perception of a connection between man and
nature is decidedly temporary and subjective.

    In the end, what we see in "Birches" and in "Two Look   **Conclusion**
at Two" is Frost not so much reconciling the disconnect between
man and nature, and certainly not pretending the gap does not
exist, but rather acknowledging the gap and using the space of
the separation as an area for the imagination to play and thus
transport us *toward* something better. The speaker in "Birches"
says as much when he claims that the best way to go is to
"climb black branches up a snow-white trunk / *Toward* heaven,
till the tree could bear no more" (55-56). And in "Two Look at
Two," the distance between nature and man becomes the space of
a subjective, imaginary transcendence. While the deer of "Two
Look at Two" perceive nothing out of the ordinary in their
encounter, man uses the encounter to imagine a connection.
That, Frost is saying, is food for the spirit, allowing us to
continue when, as he says in "Birches," "Truth [breaks] in /
With all her matter-of-fact" (21-22). Though "the world of
nature appearing in [Frost's poems] may resist man's attempts
to order it," as John J. Conder has written (44), Frost
nonetheless presents the attempt itself as redeeming.
"Political freedom is nothing to me," Frost writes in "The
Figure a Poem Makes," his 1939 Preface to the first edition of
his collected poems, "I bestow it right and left. All I would
keep for myself is the freedom of my material—the condition
of body and mind now and then to summons aptly from the vast   **Primary source**
                                                                   used to conclude
chaos of all I have lived through" (34).   **discussion**

Tanguay 6

Works Cited

Bidney, Martin. "The Secretive-Playful Epiphanies of Robert
    Frost: Solitude, Companionship, and the Ambivalent
    Imagination." <u>The Wadsworth Casebook for Reading, Research,</u>
    <u>and Writing: Robert Frost: A Collection of Poems.</u> Ed.
    Robert C. Petersen. Boston: Wadsworth, 2004. 58–66.

Bracker, Milton. "He Himself Is Perhaps the Biggest Metaphor of
    All." <u>The Wadsworth Casebook for Reading, Research, and</u>
    <u>Writing: Robert Frost: A Collection of Poems.</u> Ed. Robert C.
    Petersen. Boston: Wadsworth, 2004. 42–48.

Conder, John J. "'After Apple-Picking': Frost's Troubled
    Sleep." <u>The Wadsworth Casebook for Reading, Research, and</u>
    <u>Writing: Robert Frost: A Collection of Poems.</u> Ed. Robert C.
    Petersen. Boston: Wadsworth, 2004. 48–57.

Frost, Robert. "The Figure a Poem Makes." <u>The Wadsworth</u>
    <u>Casebook for Reading, Research, and Writing: Robert Frost:</u>
    <u>A Collection of Poems.</u> Ed. Robert C. Petersen. Boston:
    Wadsworth, 2004. 37–39.

Lentricchia, Frank. <u>Robert Frost: Modern Poetics and the</u>
    <u>Landscapes of Self</u>. Durham: Duke UP, 1975.

Link, Eric Carl. "Nature's Extra-Vagrants: Frost and Thoreau in
    the Maine Woods." <u>Papers on Language and Literature</u> 33.2
    (1997): 182–97.

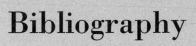

Bibliography

$\bigvee\bigvee$ hat follows are sources useful to those interested in coming to grips with Frost's ideas, his poetic practice, and particular poems themselves. The bibliography offers interviews with Frost, biographical studies and collections of letters, and book-length studies of the poet's entire output. There are also articles dealing with narrower topics, including at least one about each of the poems in this Casebook. Nothing has been reprinted from *The Explicator*, which contains many short pieces on Frost's poems. Students might look there for more detailed readings, and they might also look at *The Robert Frost Review*, a scholarly journal devoted to the poet's work.

Works by Robert Frost

ESSAYS, INTERVIEWS, AND LETTERS

Barry, Elaine, ed. Robert Frost on Writing. New Brunswick, NJ: Rutgers UP, 1973.

Francis, Robert. Frost: A Time to Talk: Conversations and Indiscretions Recorded by Robert Francis. Amherst: U of Massachusetts P, 1972.

Grade, Arnold, ed. Family Letters of Robert and Elinor Frost. Foreword by Lesley Frost. Albany: SUNY P, 1972.

Lathem, Edward Connery, ed. Interviews with Robert Frost. New York: Holt, 1966.

The Letters of Robert Frost to Louis Untermeyer. New York: Holt, 1963.

Morrison, Kathleen. Robert Frost: A Pictorial Chronicle. New York: Holt, 1974.

Thompson, Lawrance. Selected Letters of Robert Frost. New York: Holt, 1964.

POETRY AND DRAMA

Frost, Robert. A Boy's Will. London: Nutt, 1913.

———. North of Boston. London: Nutt, 1914.

———. Mountain Interval. New York: Holt, 1916.

———. New Hampshire. New York: Holt, 1923.

———. West-Running Brook. New York: Holt, 1928.

———. Collected Poems. New York: Holt, 1930.

———. A Further Range. New York: Holt, 1936.

———. Collected Poems. New York: Holt, 1939.

————. A Witness Tree. New York: Holt, 1942.

————. A Masque of Reason. New York: Holt, 1945.

————. A Masque of Mercy. New York: Holt, 1947.

————. Steeple Bush. New York: Holt, 1947.

————. Complete Poems of Robert Frost 1949. New York: Holt, 1949.

————. In The Clearing. New York: Holt, 1962.

————. Collected Poems, Prose, and Plays. Ed. Richard Poirier and Mark Richardson. New York: Lib. of Amer., 1995.

Reference

Cramer, Jeffrey C. Robert Frost among His Poems: A Literary Companion to the Poet's Own Biographical Contexts and Associations. Jefferson, NC: McFarland, 1996.

Lathem, Edward Connery, ed. A Concordance to the Poetry of Robert Frost. New York: Holt, 1971.

Lentricchia, Frank, and Melissa Christensen Lentricchia. Robert Frost: A Bibliography, 1913–1974. Metuchen, NJ: Scarecrow, 1976.

Potter, James L. Robert Frost Handbook. University Park: Pennsylvania State UP, 1980.

Van Egmond, Peter. The Critical Reception of Robert Frost. Boston: Hall, 1974.

————. Robert Frost: A Reference Guide, 1974–1990. Boston: Hall, 1991.

Biography

Burnshaw, Stanley. Robert Frost Himself. New York: Braziller, 1986.

Cox, Sidney. A Swinger of Birches: A Portrait of Robert Frost. Introduction by Robert Frost. New York: New York UP, 1957.

Francis, Lesley Lee. The Frost Family's Adventure in Poetry: Sheer Morning Gladness at the Brim. Columbia: U of Missouri P, 1994.

Parini, Jay. Robert Frost: A Life. New York: Holt, 1999.

Pritchard, William H. Frost: A Literary Life Reconsidered. New York: Oxford UP, 1984.

Reeve, F. D. Robert Frost in Russia. Boston: Little, 1963.

Sergeant, Elizabeth Shepley. Robert Frost: The Trial by Existence. New York: Holt, 1960.

Thompson, Lawrance, and R. H. Winnick. Robert Frost: A Biography. Condensed by Edward Connery Lathem. New York: Holt, 1982.

Literary and Cultural Background

Bloom, Harold. Figures of Capable Imagination. New York: Seabury, 1976.

Donoghue, Denis. Connoisseurs of Chaos: Ideas of Order in Modern American Poetry. New York: Macmillan, 1965.

Rexroth, Kenneth. American Poetry in the Twentieth Century. New York: Herder, 1971.

Sutton, Walter. American Free Verse: The Modern Revolution in Poetry. New York: New Directions, 1973.

Vendler, Helen. The Music of What Happens: Poems, Poets, Critics. Cambridge: Harvard UP, 1988.

———, ed. Voices and Visions: The Poet in America. New York: Random, 1987.

Criticism of Frost's Poetry

BOOK LENGTH STUDIES

Bagby, George F. Frost and the Book of Nature. Knoxville: U of Tennessee P, 1993.

Barry, Elaine. Robert Frost. New York: Unger, 1973.

Bloom, Harold, ed. Robert Frost: Modern Critical Views. New York: Chelsea, 1986.

Borroff, Marjorie. Language and the Poet: Verbal Artistry in Frost, Stevens, and Moore. Chicago: U of Chicago P, 1979.

Brodsky, Joseph, Seamus Heaney, and Derek Walcott. Homage to Robert Frost. New York: Farrar, 1996.

Brower, Reuben A. The Poetry of Robert Frost: Constellations of Intention. New York: Oxford UP, 1963.

Cook, Reginald. Robert Frost: Living Voice. Amherst: U of Massachusetts P, 1974.

Cox, James M., ed. Robert Frost: A Collection of Critical Essays. Englewood Cliffs, NJ: Prentice, 1962.

Frost: Centennial Essays. Ed. Jac Tharpe. Jackson: UP of Mississippi, 1974.

Gerber, Philip C., ed. Critical Essays on Robert Frost. Boston: Hall, 1982.

———. Robert Frost. 2nd ed. Boston: Twayne, 1982.

Greenberg, Robert A., and James G. Hepburn, eds. Robert Frost: An Introduction—Poems, Reviews, Criticism. New York: Holt, 1961.

Greiner, Donald J. Robert Frost: The Poet and His Critics. Chicago: Amer. Lib. Assn., 1974.

Hall, Dorothy Judd. Robert Frost: Contours of Belief. Athens: Ohio UP, 1984.

Harris, Kathryn Gibbs, ed. Robert Frost: Studies of the Poetry. Boston: Hall, 1979.

Hass, Robert Bernard. Going by Contraries: Robert Frost's Conflict with Science. Charlottesville: UP of Virginia, 2002.

Hoffman, Tyler. Robert Frost and the Politics of Poetry. Forward by Jay Parini. Hanover, NH: UP of New England, 2001.

Holland, Norman. The Brain of Robert Frost: A Cognitive Approach to Literature. New York: Routledge, 1988.

Kemp, John C. Robert Frost and New England: The Poet as Regionalist. Princeton: Princeton UP, 1979.

Kearns, Katherine. Robert Frost and a Poetics of Appetite. Cambridge Studies in American Literature and Culture. Cambridge: Cambridge UP, 1994.

Lentricchia, Frank. Robert Frost: Modern Poetics and the Landscape of the Self. Durham: Duke UP, 1975.

Lynen, John F. The Pastoral Art of Robert Frost. New Haven: Yale UP, 1960.

Mertins, Louis. Robert Frost: Life and Talks—Walking. Norman: U of Oklahoma P, 1965.

Monteiro, George. Robert Frost and the New England Renaissance. Lexington: UP of Kentucky, 1988.

Nitchie, George W. Human Values in the Poetry of Robert Frost: A Study of a Poet's Convictions. Durham, NC: Duke UP, 1960.

Oster, Judith. Toward Robert Frost: The Reader and the Poet. Athens: U of Georgia P, 1991.

Poirier, Richard. Robert Frost: The Work of Knowing. New York: Oxford UP, 1977.

Richardson, Mark. The Ordeal of Robert Frost: The Poet and His Politics. Urbana: U of Illinois P, 1997.

Squires, Radcliffe. The Major Themes of Robert Frost. Ann Arbor: U of Michigan P, 1963.

Tharpe, Jac, ed. Frost: Centennial Essays II. Jackson: UP of Mississippi, 1976.

———, ed. Frost: Centennial Essays III. Jackson: UP of Mississippi, 1978.

Thompson, Lawrance. Fire and Ice: The Art and Thought of Robert Frost. New York: Russell, 1961.

Timmerman, John H. Robert Frost: The Ethics of Ambiguity. Lewisburg: Bucknell UP, 2002.

Wilcox, Earl J., ed. His "Incalculable" Influence on Others: Essays on Robert Frost in Our Time. ELS Monograph Series, Number 63. Victoria, BC: U of Victoria, 1994.

ESSAYS IN PERIODICALS OR IN COLLECTIONS

Auden, W. H. "Robert Frost." The Dyer's Hand and Other Essays. New York: Random, 1962. 337–53.

Bacon, Helen. "For Girls: From 'Birches' to 'Wild Grapes.'" Yale Review 67 (1977): 13–29.

Baym, Nina. "An Approach to Robert Frost's Nature Poetry." American Quarterly 17 (1965): 713–23.

Bieganowski, Ronald. "Sense of Place and Religious Consciousness." Robert Frost: Studies of the Poetry. Ed. Kathryn Gibbs Harris. Boston: Hall, 1979. 29–47.

Brooks, Cleanth. "Frost and Nature." Robert Frost: The Man and the Poet. Ed. Earl J. Wilcox. Winthrop Studies on Major American Writers. Rock Hill, SC: Winthrop Coll., 1981. 1–18.

Chabot, C. Barry. "The 'Melancholy Dualism' of Robert Frost." Review of Existential Psychology and Psychiatry 13.1 (1974): 42–56.

Chamberlain, William. "The Emersonianism of Robert Frost." Emerson Society Quarterly 57.4 (1969): 61–66.

Cox, James M. "Robert Frost and the End of the New England Line." Frost: Centennial Essays. Ed. Jac Tharpe. Jackson: UP of Mississippi, 1974. 545–61.

Dendinger, Lloyd N. "Emerson's Influence on Frost through Howells." Frost: Centennial Essays. Ed. Jac Tharpe. Jackson: UP of Mississippi, 1974. 265–274.

Fitzgerald, Gregory, and Paul Ferguson. "The Frost Tradition: A Conversation with William Meredith." Southwest Review 57 (1972): 108–17.

Francis, Lesley Lee. "Between Poets: Robert Frost and Harriet Monroe." South Carolina Review 19 (1987): 2–15.

Fraser, Russell. "Frost in the Waste Land." The Sewanee Review 106.1 (1998): 46–67.

French, Warren. "'The Death of the Hired Man': Modernism and Transcendence." Frost: Centennial Essays III. Ed. Jac Tharpe. Jackson: UP of Mississippi, 1978. 383–401.

Garrison, Joseph M., Jr. " 'Our Singing Strength': The Texture of Voice in the Poetry of Robert Frost." Frost: Centennial Essays. Ed. Jac Tharpe. Jackson: UP of Mississippi, 1974. 340–350.

Gelpi, Albert. "Robert Frost: The Clearing in the Words." Gone Into If Not Explained: Essays on the Poems of Robert Frost. Ed. Greg Kuzma. Crete, NE: Best Cellar Press, 1976.

Greiner, Donald J. "The Difference Mode for Prosody." Robert Frost: Studies of the Poetry. Ed. Kathryn Gibbs Harris. Boston: Hall, 1979. 1–16.

Hall, Dorothy Judd. "The Height of Feeling Free: Frost and Bergson." Texas Quarterly 19.1 (1976): 128–43.

Hart, Jeffrey. "Frost and Eliot." Sewanee Review 84 (1976): 425–47.

Howe, Irving. "Robert Frost: A Momentary Stay." A World More Attractive: A View of Modern Literature and Politics. New York: Horizon, 1963. 144–57.

Kearns, Katherine. " 'The Place is the Asylum': Women and Nature in Robert Frost's Poetry." American Literature 59.2 (1987): 190–210.

Kern, Robert. "Frost and Modernism." American Literature 60.1 (1988): 1–16.

Lentricchia, Frank. "Experience as Meaning: Robert Frost's 'Mending Wall.' " CEA Critic 34.4 (1972): 8–12.

———. "Robert Frost and Modern Literary Theory." Frost: Centennial Essays. Ed. Jac Tharpe. Jackson: UP of Mississippi, 1974. 315–32.

Lieber, Todd M. "Robert Frost and Wallace Stevens: 'What to Make of a Diminished Thing.' " American Literature 47.1 (1975): 64–83.

Liebman, Sheldon W. "Robert Frost: On the Dialectics of Poetry." American Literature 52.2 (1980): 264–78.

Link, Eric Carl. "Nature's Extra-Vagrants: Frost and Thoreau in the Maine Woods." Papers on Language and Literature 33.2 (1997): 182–97.

Marcus, Mordecai. "Psychoanalytic Approaches to 'Mending Wall.' " Robert Frost: Studies of the Poetry. Ed. Kathryn Gibbs Harris. Boston: Hall, 1979. 178–90.

Mason, Julian. "Frost's Conscious Accommodation of Contraries." CEA Critic 38.3 (1976): 26–32.

Miller, Lewis H. "The Poet as Swinger: Fact and Fancy in Robert Frost." Criticism 16 (Winter 1974): 58–72.

Montiero, George. "Emily Dickinson and Robert Frost." Prairie Schooner 51 (1977): 369–86.

Moore, Richard. "Of Form, Closed and Open: With Glances at Frost and Williams." Iowa Review 17.3 (1987): 86–103.

Mulder, William. "Seeing 'New-Englandly': Planes of Perception in Emily Dickinson and Robert Frost." New England Quarterly 52 (1979): 550–59.

Oelschlager, Fritz. "Fences Make Neighbors: Process, Identity, and Ego in Robert Frost's 'Mending Wall.'" Arizona Quarterly 40 (1984): 242–54.

Pearce, Roy Harvey. "Frost." The Continuity of American Poetry. Princeton: Princeton UP, 1961. 271–83.

Perkins, David. "Robert Frost." A History of Modern Poetry: From the 1890s to the High Modernist Mode. Cambridge: Harvard UP, 1976. 227–51.

Poirier, Richard. "Robert Frost." Voices and Visions: The Poet in America. Ed. Helen Vendler. New York: Random, 1987. 90–121.

Replogle, Justin. "Vernacular Poetry: Frost to Frank O'Hara." Twentieth Century Literature 24 (1978): 137–53.

Ruderman, Judith. "Milton's Choices: Styron's Use of Robert Frost's Poetry in Lie Down in Darkness." College Language Association Journal 27 (1983): 141–51.

Sanders, David A. "Words in the Rush of Everything to Waste: A Poetic Theme in Frost." South Carolina Review 17 (1974): 34–37.

Scheele, Roy. "The Laborious Dream: Frost's 'After Apple-Picking.'" Gone Into If Not Explained: Essays on the Poems of Robert Frost. Ed. Greg Kuzma. Crete, NE: Best Cellar Press, 1976.

Schwartz, Delmore. "The Present State of Poetry." American Poetry at Mid-Century. Ed. John Crowe Ransom, Delmore Schwartz, and John Hall Wheelock. Washington, DC: Lib. of Congress, 1958. 15–31.

Sheehy, Donald G. " 'Not quite all, my dear': Gender and Voice in Frost." Texas Studies in Literature and Language 36.4 (1994): 403–30.

Sokol, B. J. "What Went Wrong between Robert Frost and Ezra Pound?" New England Quarterly 49 (1976): 521–41.

Toliver, Harold E. "Frost's Enclosures and Clearings." Pastoral: Forms and Attitudes. Berkeley: U of California P, 1971. 334–60.

Trilling, Lionel. "A Speech on Robert Frost: A Cultural Episode." Partisan Review 26 (1959): 445–52.

Untermeyer, Louis. "Robert Frost." American Poetry Since 1900. New York: Holt, 1923. 15–41.

Van Doren, Mark. "The Permanence of Robert Frost." The Private Reader: Selected Articles and Reviews. New York: Holt, 1942. 87–96.

Waggoner, Hyatt H. "Robert Frost: The Strategic Retreat." The Heel of Elohim: Science and Values in Modern American Poetry. Norman: U of Oklahoma P, 1950. 41–60.

Warren, Robert Penn. "The Themes of Robert Frost." Michigan Alumnus Quarterly Review 54 (1947): 1–11.
Watkins, Floyd C. "Going and Coming Back: Robert Frost's Religious Poetry." South Atlantic Quarterly 73 (1974): 445–59.
Watts, Harold H. "Robert Frost and the Interrupted Dialogue." American Literature 27 (1955): 69–87.
Wyatt, David. "Frost and the Grammar of Motion." Southern Review 16.1 (1980): 86–99.

Audio-Visual Resources

Matazzoni, Joe, ed. Robert Frost: Poems, Life, Legacy. CD-ROM. New York: Holt, 1997.
Robert Frost. Voices and Visions Series. PBS Adult Learning Services, 1988.

Internet Resources

"A Frost Bouquet: Robert Frost, His Family, and the Clifton Waller Barrett Library of American Literature". An Exhibition in the Tracy W. McGregor Room, March 1, 1996–June 1, 1996. 22 Feb. 1999. Rector and Visitors of the U of VA. 9 July 2003 <http://www.lib.virginia.edu/speccol/exhibits/frost/home.html>.
Heath Online Instructor's Guide: Robert Frost (1874–1963). Ed. James Guimond. 20 June 2003 <http://www.georgetown.edu/faculty/bassr/heath/syllabuild/iguide/frost.html>.
Modern American Poetry: An Online Journal and Multimedia Companion to Anthology of Modern American Poetry (Oxford, 2000). Ed. Cary Nelson. 2000. Dept of English, U of Illinois at Urbana-Champaign. 25 June 2003 <http://www.english.uiuc.edu/maps>.
"Robert Frost." The Academy of American Poets. 4 Apr 2002. 25 June 2003 <http://www.poets.org/poets/poets.cfm>.
Robert Frost House (1875). 2000. Amherst Common. 9 July 2003 <http://www.amherstcommon.com/walking_tour/robfrost.html>.
Robert Frost on the Web. 9 July 2003 <http://www.amherstcommon.com/walking_tour/frost.html>.
The Robert Frost Web Page. Ed. Jay Michalowski, Tim Kroemer, and Stephen J. Goodson. 20 April 1999. 25 June 2003 <http://www.robertfrost.org>.

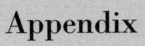

Appendix

A Guide to MLA Documentation Style

Documentation is the acknowledgment of information from outside sources that you use in your paper. In general, give credit to your sources whenever you quote, paraphrase, summarize, or in any way incorporate borrowed information or ideas into your work. Not to do so—on purpose or by accident—is to commit **plagiarism,** to appropriate the intellectual property of others. By following accepted conventions of documentation, you not only help avoid plagiarism, but you show your readers that you write with care and precision. In addition, you enable them to distinguish your ideas from those of your sources and, if they wish, to locate and consult the sources you cite.

Not all ideas from your sources need to be documented. You can assume that certain information—facts from encyclopedias, textbooks, newspapers, magazines, and dictionaries, or even from television and radio—is common knowledge. Even if the information is new to you, it need not be documented as long as it is found in several reference sources and as long as you do not use the exact wording of your source. Information that is in dispute or that is the original contribution of a particular person, however, *must* be documented. You need not, for example, document the fact that Arthur Miller's *Death of a Salesman* was first performed in 1949 or that it won a Pulitzer Prize for drama. (You could find this information in any current encyclopedia.) You would, however, have to document a critic's interpretation of a performance or a scholar's analysis of an early draft of the play, even if you do not use your source's exact words.

Students writing about literature use the documentation style recommended by the Modern Language Association (MLA), a professional organization of more than 25,000 teachers and students of English and other languages. This style of documentation has three parts: *parenthetical references* in the text, a *works-cited list* at the end of the paper, and *content notes.*

PARENTHETICAL REFERENCES IN THE TEXT

MLA documentation style uses parenthetical references within the text to refer to an alphabetical works-cited list at the end of the paper. A parenthetical reference should contain just enough information to guide readers to the appropriate entry on your works-cited list. A typical

parenthetical reference consists of the author's last name and a page number.

> Gwendolyn Brooks uses the sonnet form to create poems that have a wide social and aesthetic range (Williams 972).

If you use more than one source by the same author, include a shortened title in the parenthetical reference.

> Brooks knows not only Shakespeare, Spenser, and Milton, but also the full range of African-American poetry (Williams, "Brooks's Way" 972).

If you mention the author's name or the title of the work in your paper, only a page reference is needed.

> According to Gladys Margaret Williams in "Gwendolyn Brooks's Way with the Sonnet," Brooks combines a sensitivity to poetic forms with a depth of emotion appropriate for her subject matter (972-73).

SAMPLE PARENTHETICAL REFERENCES

An entire work

> August Wilson's play *Fences* treats many themes frequently expressed in modern drama.

When citing an entire work, state the name of the author in your paper instead of in a parenthetical reference.

A work by two or three authors

> Myths cut across boundaries and cultural spheres and reappear in strikingly similar forms from country to country (Feldman and Richardson 124).

> The effect of a work of literature depends on the audience's predispositions that derive from membership in various social groups (Hovland, Janis, and Kelley 87).

A work by more than three authors

> Hawthorne's short stories frequently use a combination of allegorical and symbolic methods (Guerin et al. 91).

The abbreviation *et al.* is Latin for "and others."

A work in an anthology

> In his essay "Flat and Round Characters," E. M. Forster
> distinguishes between one-dimensional characters and those that
> are well developed (Stevick 223-31).

The parenthetical reference cites the anthology (edited by Stevick) that contains Forster's essay; full information about the anthology appears in the list of works cited.

A work with volume and page numbers

> Critics consider The Zoo Story to be one of Albee's best plays
> (Eagleton 2:17).

An indirect source

> Wagner observed that myth and history stood before him "with
> opposing claims" (qtd. in Winkler 10).

The abbreviation *qtd. in* ("quoted in") indicates that the quoted material was not taken from the original source.

A play with numbered lines

> "Give thy thoughts no tongue," says Polonius, "Nor any
> unproportioned thought his act" (*Ham.* 1.3.64-65).

The parentheses contain the act, scene, and line numbers (in arabic numerals), separated by periods. When included in parenthetical references, titles of the books of the Bible and well-known literary works are often abbreviated—*Gen.* for *Genesis* and *Ado* for *Much Ado about Nothing,* for example.

A poem

> "I muse my life-long hate, and without flinch / I bear it nobly
> as I live my part," says Claude McKay in his bitterly ironic poem
> "The White City" (lines 3-4).

Notice that a slash (/) is used to separate lines of poetry run in with the text. (The slash is preceded and followed by one space.) The parenthetical reference cites the lines quoted. Include the word *line* or *lines* for the first reference but just the numbers for subsequent references.

An electronic source

If you are citing a source from the Internet or from an online service to which your library subscribes, remember that these sources frequently do not contain page numbers. If the source uses paragraph, section, or screen numbers, use the abbreviation "par." "sec.," or the full word "screen."

> The earliest type of movie censoring came in the form of licensing fees, and in Deer River, Minnesota, "a licensing fee of $200 was deemed not excessive for a town of 1000" (Ernst, par. 20).

If the source has no page numbers or markers of any kind, cite the entire work. (When readers get to the works-cited list, they will be able to determine the nature of the source.)

> In her article "Limited Horizons," Lynne Cheney says that schools do best when students read literature not for what it tells them about the workplace, but for its insights into the human condition.

> Because of its parody of communism, the film *Antz* is actually an adult film masquerading as a child's tale (Clemin).

THE LIST OF WORKS CITED

Parenthetical references refer to a **works-cited list** that includes all the sources you refer to in your paper. Begin the works-cited list on a new page, continuing the page numbers of the paper. For example, if the text of the paper ends on page 6, the works-cited section will begin on page 7.

Informal Documentation

Sometimes, when you are writing a paper that includes quotations from a single source that the entire class has read, or if all your sources are from your textbook, your instructor may give you permission to use *informal documentation*. Because both the instructor and the class are familiar with the sources, you supply the authors' last names and page numbers in parentheses but do not include a works-cited list.

Center the title *Works Cited* one inch from the top of the page. Arrange entries alphabetically, according to the last name of each author. Use the first word of the title if the author is unknown (articles—*a, an,* and *the*—

at the beginning of a title are not considered first words). To conserve space, publishers' names are abbreviated—for example, *U. of California P* (for University of California Press). Double-space the entire works-cited list between and within entries. Begin typing each entry at the left margin, and indent subsequent lines five spaces (or one-half inch). Each works-cited entry has three divisions—author, title, and publishing information—separated by periods. The *MLA Handbook for Writers of Research Papers* shows a single space after all end punctuation.

Below is a directory of the sample entries that follow.

Entries for Books

1. A book by a single author
2. A book by two or three authors
3. A book by more than three authors
4. Two or more works by the same author
5. An edited book
6. A book with a volume number
7. A short story, poem, or play in a collection of the author's work
8. A short story in an anthology
9. A poem in an anthology
10. A play in an anthology
11. An article in an anthology
12. More than one selection from the same anthology
13. A translation

Entries for Articles

14. An article in a journal with continuous pagination throughout an annual volume
15. An article with separate pagination in each issue
16. An article in a magazine
17. An article in a daily newspaper
18. An article in a reference book

Entries for Other Sources

19. A film or videocassette
20. An interview
21. A lecture or an address

Entries for Electronic Sources (Internet)

22. A scholarly project or information database on the Internet
23. A document within a scholarly project or information database on the Internet
24. A personal site on the Internet
25. A book on the Internet
26. An article in a scholarly journal on the Internet
27. An article in an encyclopedia on the Internet
28. An article in a newspaper on the Internet
29. An article in a magazine on the Internet
30. A painting or photograph on the Internet
31. An e-mail
32. An online posting

Entries for Electronic Sources (Subscription Service)

33. A scholarly journal article with separate pagination in each issue from a subscription service
34. A scholarly journal article with continuous pagination throughout an annual volume from a subscription service
35. A monthly magazine article from a subscription service
36. A newspaper article from a subscription service
37. A reference book article from a subscription service
38. A dictionary definition from a subscription service

Entries for Other Electronic Sources

39. A nonperiodical publication on CD-ROM
40. A periodical publication on CD-ROM

Entries for Books

1. *A book by a single author*

Kingston, Maxine Hong. The Woman Warrior: Memoirs of a Girlhood
among Ghosts. New York: Knopf, 1976.

2. *A book by two or three authors*

Feldman, Burton, and Robert D. Richardson. The Rise of Modern
Mythology. Bloomington: Indiana UP, 1972.

Notice that only the *first* author's name is in reverse order.

3. *A book by more than three authors*

Guerin, Wilfred, et al., eds. A Handbook of Critical Approaches
to Literature. 3rd ed. New York: Harper, 1992.

Instead of using *et al.*, you may list all the authors' names in the order in which they appear on the title page.

4. *Two or more works by the same author*

Novoa, Juan-Bruce. Chicano Authors: Inquiry by Interview. Austin:
U of Texas P, 1980.
− − − . "Themes in Rudolfo Anaya's Work." Address given at New
Mexico State University, Las Cruces. 11 Apr. 1987.

List two or more works by the same author in alphabetical order by title. Include the author's full name in the first entry; use three unspaced hyphens followed by a period to take the place of the author's name in second and subsequent entries.

5. *An edited book*

Oosthuizen, Ann, ed. Sometimes When It Rains: Writings by South
African Women. New York: Pandora, 1987.

Notice that here the abbreviation *ed.* stands for *editor*.

6. *A book with a volume number*

When all the volumes of a multivolume work have the same title, list the number of the volume you used.

Eagleton, T. Allston. A History of the New York Stage. Vol. 2.
Englewood Cliffs: Prentice, 1987.

When each volume of a multivolume work has a separate title, list the title of the volume you used.

> Durant, Will, and Ariel Durant. <u>The Age of Napoleon: A History of</u>
> <u>European Civilization from 1789 to 1815</u>. New York: Simon,
> 1975.

The Age of Napoleon is volume 2 of *The Story of Civilization.* You need not provide information about the work as a whole.

7. *A short story, poem, or play in a collection of the author's work*

> Gordimer, Nadine. "Once upon a Time." <u>"Jump" and Other Stories</u>.
> New York: Farrar, 1991. 23-30.

8. *A short story in an anthology*

> Salinas, Marta. "The Scholarship Jacket." <u>Nosotros: Latina</u>
> <u>Literature Today</u>. Ed. Maria del Carmen Boza, Beverly Silva,
> and Carmen Valle. Binghamton: Bilingual, 1986. 68-70.

Note that here the abbreviation *Ed.* stands for *Edited by*. The inclusive page numbers follow the year of publication.

9. *A poem in an anthology*

> Simmerman, Jim. "Child's Grave, Hale County, Alabama." <u>The</u>
> <u>Pushcart Prize, X: Best of the Small Presses</u>. Ed. Bill
> Henderson. New York: Penguin, 1986. 198-99.

10. *A play in an anthology*

> Hughes, Langston. <u>Mother and Child. Black Drama Anthology</u>. Ed.
> Woodie King and Ron Miller. New York: NAL, 1986. 399-406.

11. *An article in an anthology*

> Forster, E. M. "Flat and Round Characters." <u>The Theory of the</u>
> <u>Novel</u>. Ed. Philip Stevick. New York: Free, 1980. 223-31.

12. *More than one selection from the same anthology*

If you are using more than one selection from an anthology, cite the anthology in a separate entry. Then, list each individual selection separately, including the author and title of the selection, the anthology editor's last name, and the inclusive page numbers.

Baxter, Charles. "Gryphon." Kirszner and Mandell 136-47.

Kirszner, Laurie G., and Stephen R. Mandell, eds. Literature:
Reading, Reacting, Writing. 5th ed. Boston: Wadsworth, 2004.

Rich, Adrienne. "Diving into the Wreck." Kirszner and Mandell
1019-21.

13. *A translation*

Carpentier, Alejo. Reasons of State. Trans. Francis Partridge.
New York: Norton, 1976.

Entries for Articles

Article citations include the author's name; the title of the article (in quotation marks); the name of the periodical (underlined); and the pages on which the full article appears (without the abbreviations *p.* or *pp.*).

14. *An article in a journal with continuous pagination throughout an annual volume*

LeGuin, Ursula K. "American Science Fiction and the Other."
Science Fiction Studies 2 (1975): 208-10.

15. *An article with separate pagination in each issue*

Grossman, Robert. "The Grotesque in Faulkner's 'A Rose for
Emily.'" Mosaic 20.3 (1987): 40-55.

Note that *20.3* signifies volume 20, issue 3.

16. *An article in a magazine*

Milosz, Czeslaw. "A Lecture." The New Yorker 22 June 1992: 32.
"Solzhenitsyn: An Artist Becomes an Exile." Time 25 Feb. 1974:
34+.

Note that 34+ indicates that the article appears on pages that are not consecutive; in this case, the article begins on page 34 and continues on page 37. An article with no listed author is entered by title on the works-cited list.

17. *An article in a daily newspaper*

Oates, Joyce Carol. "When Characters from the Page Are Made Flesh
on the Screen." New York Times 23 Mar. 1986, late ed.: C1+.

C1+ indicates that the article begins on page 1 of Section C and continues on a subsequent page.

18. *An article in a reference book*

Do not include publication information for well-known reference books.

> "Dance Theatre of Harlem." The New Encyclopaedia Britannica:
> Micropaedia. 15th ed. 1987.

Include publication information when citing reference books that are not well known.

> Grimstead, David. "Fuller, Margaret Sarah." Encyclopedia of
> American Biography. Ed. John A. Garraty. New York: Harper,
> 1974.

Entries for Other Sources

19. *A film or videocassette*

> "A Worn Path." By Eudora Welty. Dir. John Reid and Claudia
> Velasco. Perf. Cora Lee Day and Conchita Ferrell.
> Videocassette. Wadsworth, 1994.

20. *An interview*

> Brooks, Gwendolyn. "An Interview with Gwendolyn Brooks."
> Triquarterly 60 (1984): 405-10.

21. *A lecture or an address*

> Novoa, Juan-Bruce. "Themes in Rudolfo Anaya's Work." Literature
> Colloquium. New Mexico State University. Las Cruces. 11 Apr.
> 1987.

Entries for Electronic Sources (Internet)

MLA style recognizes relevant publication information is not always available for electronic sources. Include in your citation whatever information you can reasonably obtain. Include both the date of the electronic publication (if available) and the date you accessed the source. In addition, include the URL (electronic address) in angle brackets. If you have to carry the URL over to the next line, divide it after a slash. If the URL is excessively long, use just the URL of the site's search page, or use the URL of the site's home page, followed by the word *path* and a colon and then the sequence of links to follow.

22. *A scholarly project or information database on the Internet*

> Philadelphia Writers Project. Ed. Miriam Kotzen Green. May 1998.
> Drexel U. 12 June 1999 <http://www.Drexel.edu/letrs/wwp/>.

23. *A document within a scholarly project or information database on the Internet*

> "D-Day: June 7th, 1944." The History Channel Online. 1999.
> History Channel. 7 June 1999 <http://historychannel.com/
> thisday/today/997690.html>.

24. *A personal site on the Internet*

> Yerkes, James. Chiron's Forum: John Updike Home Page. 23 June
> 1999. 30 June 1999 <http://www.users.fast.net/~joyerkers/
> item9.html>.

25. *A book on the Internet*

> Douglass, Frederick. My Bondage and My Freedom. Boston: 1855. 8
> June 1999 <gopher://gopher.vt.edu:10024/22/178/3>.

26. *An article in a scholarly journal on the Internet*

> Dekoven, Marianne. "Utopias Limited: Post-Sixties and Postmodern
> American Fiction." Modern Fiction Studies 41.1 (1995): 13 pp.
> 17 Mar. 1999 <http://muse.jhu.edu/journals/mfs.v041/
> 41.1dwkovwn.html>.

When you cite information from the print version of an electronic source, include the publication information for the printed source, the number of pages or paragraphs (if available), and the date of access.

27. *An article in an encyclopedia on the Internet*

> "Hawthorne, Nathaniel." Britannica Online. Vers. 98.2. Apr. 1998.
> Encyclopedia Britannica. 16 May 1998 <http://www.eb/com/
> :220>.

28. *An article in a newspaper on the Internet*

> Lohr, Steve. "Microsoft Goes to Court." New York Times on the Web
> 19 Oct. 1998. 29 Apr. 1999 <http://www.nytimes.com/web/
> docroot/library.cyber/week/1019business.html>.

29. *An article in a magazine on the Internet*

> Weiser, Jay. "The Tyranny of Informality." Time 26 Feb. 1996.
> 1 Mar. 1999 <http://www.enews.com/magazines.tnr/current/
> 022696.3.html>.

30. *A painting or photograph on the Internet*

> Lange, Dorothea, Looking at Pictures. 1936. Museum of Mod. Art,
> New York. 17 July 2000 <http://moma.org/exhibitions/
> lookingatphotographs/lang-fr.html>.

31. *An e-mail*

> Adkins, Camille. E-mail to the author. 28 June 2001.

32. *An online posting*

> Gilford, Mary. "Dog Heroes in Children's Literature." Online
> posting. 17 Mar. 1999. 12 Apr. 1999 <news:alt.animals.dogs>.

Entries for Electronic Sources (Online Subscription Service)

Online subscription services can be divided into those you subscribe to, such as America Online, and those that your college library subscribes to, such as Extended Academic ASAP, Lexis-Nexis, and Pro-Quest Direct.

To cite information from an online service to which you subscribe, you have two options. If the service provides a URL, follow the examples in entries 22 through 30. If the service enables you to use a keyword to access material, provide the keyword (following the date of access) at the end of the entry.

> "Kafka, Franz." Compton's Encyclopedia Online. Vers. 3.0. 2000.
> America Online. 8 June 2001. Keyword: Compton's.

If, instead of a keyword, you follow a series of topic labels, list them (separated by semicolons) after the word *Path*.

> "Elizabeth Adams." History Resources. 11 Nov. 2001. America
> Online. 28 Apr. 2001. Path: Research; Biology; Women in
> Science; Biographies.

To cite information from an online service to which your library subscribes, include the underlined name of the database (if known), the name of the service, the library, the date of access, and the URL of the online service's home page.

> Luckenbill, Trent. "Environmental Litigation: Down the Endless
> Corridor." Environment 17 July 2001: 34-42. ABI/INFORM
> GLOBAL. ProQuest Direct. Drexel U Lib., Philadelphia. 12 Oct.
> 2001 <http://www.umi.com/proquest>.

33. *A scholarly journal article with separate pagination in each issue from an online service*

> Schaefer, Richard J. "Editing Strategies in Television News
> Documentaries." Journal of Communication 47.4 (1997): 69-89.
> InfoTrac OneFile Plus. Gale Group Databases. Augusta R.
> Kolwyck Lib., Chattanooga, TN. 2 Oct. 2002 <http://
> library.cstcc.cc.tn.us/ref3.shtml>.

34. *A scholarly journal article with continuous pagination throughout an annual volume from an online service*

> Hudson, Nicholas. "Samuel Johnson, Urban Culture, and the
> Geography of Postfire London." Studies in English Literature
> 42 (2002): 557-80. MasterFILE Premier. EBSCOhost. Augusta R.
> Kolwyck Lib., Chattanooga, TN. 2 Oct. 2002 <http://
> library.cstcc.cc.tn.us/ref3.shtml>.

35. *A monthly magazine article from an online service*

> Livermore, Beth. "Meteorites on Ice." Astronomy July 1993: 54-58.
> Expanded Academic ASAP Plus. Gale Group Databases. Augusta R.
> Kolwyck Lib., Chattanooga, TN. 2 Oct. 2002 <http://
> library.cstcc.cc.tn.us/ref3.shtml>.

36. *A newspaper article from an online service*

> Meyer, Greg. "Answering Questions about the West Nile Virus."
> Dayton Daily News 11 July 2002: Z3-Z7. LexisNexis Academic.
> Augusta R. Kolwyck Lib., Chattanooga, TN. 2 Oct. 2002
> <http://library.cstcc.cc.tn.us/ref3.shtml>.

37. *A reference book article from an online service*

> Laird, Judith. "Geoffrey Chaucer." Cyclopedia of World Authors.
> 1997. MagillOnLiterature. EBSCOhost. Augusta R. Kolwyck Lib.,

```
Chattanooga, TN. 2 Oct. 2002 <http://library.cstcc.cc.tn.us/
ref3.shtml>.
```

38. *A dictionary definition from an online service*

```
"Migraine." Mosby's Medical, Nursing, and Allied Health
    Dictionary. 1998 ed. Health Reference Center. Gale Group
    Databases. Augusta R. Kolwyck Lib., Chattanooga, TN. 2 Oct.
    2002 <http://library.cstcc.cc.tn.us/ref3.shtml>.
```

Entries for Other Electronic Sources

39. *A nonperiodical publication on CD-ROM*

```
"Windhover." The Oxford English Dictionary. 2nd ed. CD-ROM.
    Oxford: Oxford UP, 1992.
```

40. *A periodical publication on CD-ROM*

```
Zurbach, Kate. "The Linguistic Roots of Three Terms." Linguistic
    Quarterly 37 (1994): 12-47. InfoTrac: Magazine Index Plus.
    CD-ROM. Information Access. Jan. 1996.
```

WARNING: Using information from an Internet source can be risky. Contributors are not necessarily experts, and they frequently are inaccurate or misinformed. Unless you can be certain that the information you are obtaining from these sources is reliable, do not use it. You can check the reliability of an Internet source by asking your instructor or librarian for guidance.

CONTENT NOTES

Use **content notes,** indicated by a superscript (a raised number) in the text, to cite several sources at once or to provide commentary or explanations that do not fit smoothly into your paper. The full text of these notes appears on the first numbered page following the last page of the paper. (If your paper has no content notes, the works-cited page follows the last page of the paper.) Like works-cited entries, content notes are double-spaced within and between entries. However, the first line of each explanatory note is indented five spaces (or one-half inch), and subsequent lines are flush with the left-hand margin.

To Cite Several Sources

In the paper

Surprising as it may seem, there have been many attempts to define literature.[1]

In the note

[1] For an overview of critical opinion, see Arnold 72; Eagleton 1-2; Howe 43-44; and Abrams 232-34.

To Provide Explanations

In the paper

In recent years, gothic novels have achieved great popularity.[3]

In the note

[3] Gothic novels, works written in imitation of medieval romances, originally relied on supernatural occurrences. They flourished in the late eighteenth and early nineteenth centuries.

Text Credits

"Two Look at Two," "The Need of Being Versed in Country Things," "Desert Places," "Design," and "The Gift Outright" from The Poetry of Robert Frost, Ed. Edward Connery Lathem. Copyright © 1936, 1942, 1944, 1951, 1958, 1964 by Robert Frost, © 1923, 1930, 1969 by Henry Holt and Company, © 1970 by Lesley Frost Ballantine. Reprinted by permission of Henry Holt and Company, LLC.

"The Figure a Poem Makes" from Selected Prose of Robert Frost, Ed. Hyde Cox and Edward Connery Lathem. Copyright © 1939, 1967 by Henry Holt and Company. Reprinted by permission of Henry Holt and Company, LLC.

Bidney, Martin, "The Secretive Playful Epiphanies of Robert Frost: Solitude, Companionship, and the Ambivalent Imagination" from Papers on Language and Literature, Vol. 38. Copyright © 2002. Reprinted by permission of Papers on Language and Literature and the author.

Bracker, Martin, "He Himself Is Perhaps the Biggest Metaphor of All" from Interviews with Robert Frost, Ed. Edward Connery Lathem. Copyright © 1966 by Henry Holt and Company, © 1994 by Edward Connery Lathem. Reprinted by permission of Henry Holt and Company, LLC.

Conder, John, " 'After Apple-Picking': Frost's Troubled Sleep" from Frost: Centennial Essays, Ed. Jac Tharpe. Copyright © 1974 by University Press of Mississippi. Reprinted by permission of University Press of Mississippi.

Frost, Robert, "Poetry and School" from Collected Poems, Prose, & Plays, Ed. Richard Poirier and Mark Richardson. Copyright © The Estate of Robert Frost.

Greiner, Donald J, " 'That Plain-Speaking Guy': A Conversation with James Dickey on Robert Frost" from Frost: Centennial Essays, Ed. Jac Tharpe. Copyright © 1974 by University Press of Mississippi. Reprinted by permission of University Press of Mississippi.

Meredith, William, "In Memory of Robert Frost," from Partial Accounts: New and Selected Poems. Copyright © 1988 by William Meredith.

Photo Credits

Page 3, Robert Frost at JFK's inauguration: © Bettmann/CORBIS; Page 15, Robert Frost: © Marty Lederhandler/Associated Press/AP; Page 16, young Robert Frost: © Hulton Archive/GETTY